AN INTRODUCTION
TO POETRY

AN INTRODUCTION TO POETRY
The River Sings

JEFF KNORR
Sacramento City College

Upper Saddle River, New Jersey 07458

Library of Congress Cataloging-in-Publication Data

Knorr, Jeff.
      The river sings : an introduction to poetry / Jeff Knorr.
         p. cm.
      ISBN 0-13-093292-2
         1. English language—Rhetoric—Problems, exercises, etc. 2. Poetry—History and
      criticism—Problems, exercises, etc. 3. Criticism—Authorship—Problems, exercises, etc.
      4. Poetry—Collections. 5. College readers. I. Title.

      PE1479.C7K59 2003
      808.1—dc21

                                                                            2003043348

Editor in Chief: Leah Jewell
Senior Acquisitions Editor: Carrie Brandon
Assistant Editor: Karen A. Schultz
Editorial Assistant: Jennifer Migueis
Production Editor: Melissa Scott, Carlisle Communications, Inc.
Prepress and Manufacturing Buyer: Brian Mackey
Senior Marketing Manager: Rachel Falk
Marketing Assistant: Adam Laitman
Text Permissions Specialist: Mary Dalton-Hoffman
Cover Designer: Robert Farrar-Wagner
Cover Art: Russell Chatham. Courtesy Angler Art & Gifts

For permission to use copyrighted material, grateful acknowledgment is made to the copyright
holders on pages 117-120, which are considered an extension of this copyright page.

This book was set in 10/12 Sabon by Carlisle Communications, Inc., and was printed and
bound by Courier Companies, Inc. The cover was printed by Phoenix Color Corp.

Printed in the United States of America

Pearson Education LTD.
Pearson Education Singapore, Pte. Ltd
Pearson Education, Canada, Ltd
Pearson Education—Japan
Pearson Education Australia PTY, Limited

Pearson Education North Asia Ltd
Pearson Educación de Mexico, S.A. de C.V.
Pearson Education Malaysia, Pte. Ltd
Pearson Education, Upper Saddle River,
   New Jersey

10 9 8 7 6 5 4 3 2
ISBN 0-13-093292-2

CONTENTS

PREFACE

When Prentice Hall Editor, Carrie Brandon first approached me about this book, we were sitting at a conference in Kansas City talking poetry, teaching, reading, and how we've both come to have a love for literature, language, and reading. The more we talked, the conversation drifted toward how that happened, from our parents reading to us when we were children to having teachers in our lives who made books, stories, and literature a real and powerful event. In the course of that conversation, we also talked about why so many people come out of their varied academic backgrounds with a love for reading fiction and non-fiction but not poetry. And, of course, there has been much written about this by poets like Billy Collins, Delmore Schwartz, and Julia Alvarez. And possibly Robert Pinsky's poetry project served to remedy this in some way. So, the intent of this book is to break the barrier—whatever that barrier is, as it might vary for each person— to unlock some secret inside poetry.

This book is set up to: provide a background in reading poetry, analyze poems, apply literary theory, form opinions, and offer approaches to discuss and write about poetry. But, it is also designed to teach students of poetry about how a writer works and that if we understand how a writer works we might, as a reader, feel more comfortable reading poems. So, the hope is to provide an academic experience and to cultivate a lifelong love of poetry. In his essay, "The Specialization of Poetry," Wendell Berry says that "poetry remains a specialized art, its range and influence so constricted that poets have very nearly become their own audience." With hope, there is a selection of poetry here that speaks to the reader and says *poetry is not constricted*. And my hope is that the approach to reading poetry—for academic assignments, analysis, or leisure—is one which allows for poetry to be viewed as something other than a specialized art form that is only comprehensible to poets, critics, and studied academics.

As poets, should we withdraw from responsibility all that is not comprehended in our work? Most definitely not; hence, poets ought to move toward a writing, which offers the public a view of themselves and their histories, straddling the line between accessible and challenging. Asserting that this lack of responsibility has taken place in some instances, this book seeks to offer a palette of poets and approaches to reading poems that not only offers the public as subject but hopes for it to be the welcome and comfortable audience of the art. However, do not let that statement be taken as a "sit back in your easy chair and read on, Dear Reader" comment. Rather, put on your running shoes and get ready to chase the dog.

One problem, which seems to exist in many introduction to literature survey courses, or an introduction to poetry course, is that students are not only confused by poetry, but they're uncomfortable reading it aloud—no one has spent time offering them tips on reading it but has only read it to them. Literally, students often do not know how to make it come out of their mouths. Hence, in the chapter on reading a poem, "From Page to Mouth to Ear" students have some tips on getting a poem off the page and comfortably, confidently reading. What's more, for you students, during the writing of this book I had a constant companion of a composite college student. Sometimes it was a young man and sometimes a young woman. And I had a fine "standard" composite college apartment. And it was from that apartment that I wrote with this student talking to me, looking over my shoulder and directing me. For this, I hope you find the book conversational, interesting, and different than you've encountered before. *The River Sings* is intended to be a practical guide to reading poetry. This book will help instructors illustrate that there are no secret handshakes; that poetry is not a conspiracy against the reader; and that in fact students can enjoy and be comfortable within poetic language.

ACKNOWLEDGMENTS

I would like to thank all of the writers and deceased writers' estates for their cooperation and support for this book. Moreover, I especially want to thank my editor, Carrie Brandon, for her unending enthusiasm, vision, and creativity for helping this book come to fruition and reach readers. Karen Schulz, Assistant Editor on this project, offered essential support, focus, and dedication—thank you. And thanks to Jennifer Migueis and everyone at Prentice Hall who provided support and energy to the book. I would also like to extend a sincere thank-you to all the reviewers of this book— your valuable feedback was exceptionally helpful and necessary. To friends and colleagues who kept me laughing and working—Tim Schell, Troy Myers, Kate Gray, Albert Garcia, Robin Ikegami, Kevin Stein, Virgil Suarez, Pat and Kristin Hansen, and my fishing crew in Oregon—many thanks. And finally, I want to extend deep gratitude to my wife Diane and my son Gabriel for their patience, care, and support throughout the writing of this book.

Reviewers

Liza Karlin
University of DE

Cheryl Wilson
University of DE

Bob Hogge
Weber State University

Kathy Henkins
Mt. San Antonio College

Hershman John
Maricopa CC

Millicent C. Burgas
Orange Coast College

David L. Miller, Jr
Fayetteville Tech CC

Susan Dunn West
SMSU

Matt Smith
Heartland CC

Todd Pierce
Florida State University

Virgil Suarez
Florida State University

Troy Myers
Sacramento City College

Brad E. Lucas
University of NV, Reno

Evie Miller
Idaho State University

David Brantley
Cape Fear CC

Peter Burnham
Student

Robert Xidis
JCCC

Karina Roberts
Student

Iliana Rocha
Student

Ian Latta
Student

Julie Johnson
Student

Megan Wagner
Student

AN INTRODUCTION TO POETRY

Chapter One

Survivalist Poetics

When reading poetry, whether we're an experienced reader or not, one thing is certain: Poetry ought to move us. It should knock us down with the force of a boxer. It might make us cry out loud over a page. It may move us to very simple and quiet contemplation of our own life. Poetry may slow us down in the rest of our life—make us late for work, or class, or meeting friends at a local pub. It might strike fear in us. It may confuse us to no end. And, poetry may turn us inside out without warning. When I read poetry, and when I read it with my own classes, I hope it does all of these things. Sometimes people wonder why they should care if these things happen at all. Well, one answer, simply put, is if any of the above mentioned things happen to us, we hopefully learn to live better.

"Poetry is not a luxury. It is a vital necessity of our existence. It forms the quality of light within on which we predicate our hopes and dreams toward survival and change, first made into language, then into idea, then into more tangible action."

Audre Lord

Often students ask how they should come to know the "answer to a poem—what it means." And my answer to that is twofold: 1) "So, tell me Sonia, What does that poem mean to you? Why are you reacting to it?" and 2) "remember to think about and know a bit about the author, when they might have written the work, what country or region they're from, political happenings of the time, language meaning." That's all a bit technical and it's work. Sonia, and anyone else, always has an answer, and that's important. I usually find that this answer is most likely tied to the author's meaning of the poem or a "critical" meaning of the poem. Take Sonia, for instance. In a past class, we read Jimmy Santiago Baca's poem "Green Chile," and then I asked the class to comment on this poem first from the question number 1 position. The poem discusses a relationship with a grandmother, one that has formed over food, one that has formed over heritage and generations, and about politics impinging upon the Latino culture. Let's look at the poem.

Green Chile

by Jimmy Santiago Baca

I prefer red chile over my eggs
and potatoes for breakfast.
Red chile *rastras* decorate my door
dry on my roof, and hang from eaves.
They lend open-air vegetable stands
historical grandeur, and gently swing
with an air of festive welcome.
I can hear them talking in the wind
haggard, yellowing, crisp, rasping
tongues of old men, licking the breeze.

But grandmother loves green chile.
When I visit her,
she holds the green chile pepper
in her wrinkled hands.
Ah, voluptuous, masculine,
an air of authority and youth simmers
from its swan-neck stem, tapering to a flowery
collar, fermenting resinous spice.
A well-dressed gentleman at the door
my grandmother takes sensuously in her hand
rubbing its firm glossed sides,

caressing the oily rubbery serpent,
with mouth-watering fulfillment,
fondling its curves with gentle fingers.
Its bearing magnificent and taut
as flanks of a tiger in mid leap,
she thrusts her blade
and cuts it open, with lust
on her hot mouth, sweating over the stove,
bandanna round her forehead,
mysterious passion on her face
and she serves me green chile con carne
between soft warm leaves of corn tortillas,
with beans and rice—her sacrifice
to her little prince.
I slurp from my plate
with last bit of tortilla, my mouth burns
and I hiss and drink a tall glass of cold water.

All over New Mexico, sunburned men and women
drive rickety trucks stuffed with gunny-sacks
of green chile, from Belen, Veguita, Willard, Estancia
San Antonio y Socorro, from fields
to roadside stands, you see them roasting green chile
in screen-sided homemade barrels, and for a dollar a bag
we relive this old, beautiful ritual again and again.

Well, Sonia quickly raised her hand and said, "Look, this is funny the way he starts, by saying he likes red *chile,* because I prefer it too. I mean who eats green chiles on their eggs?" She was interested, she had me interested, and Baca had her right where he wanted her. She went on. "Then he goes to his grandma's house where he's just loving this green chile she makes—then he gets kind of lustful about the chiles, which is a bit weird, but that's kind of funny too because he's got his grandma lusting over the chiles and they're hot and, oh whatever. . . ." Sonia stopped, a bit unsure of her answer now, as if she walked way off her path. What she doesn't realize is that Baca is right next to her, like a spirit. Then she stops.

Justin, a horse ranching kid from a nearby farming and logging community jumped in at the pause. "You know, I totally relate to this poem, and you know what, it is funny. Man, I never saw the humor in it until just now when Sonia was talking. Anyway, I used to go to my grandmother's house all the time for her pancakes, and. . . " He pauses. Then Justin keeps going and he's on target. "Anyway, I would actually get up early on Saturdays, even if I was out late Friday, to get all my morning farm work done so I could ditch my house and go down the road for breakfast with my grandparents. My dad always made pancakes too on Saturdays but my grandma's were better. They were this Scandinavian kind she'd had in her house for generations, and she made it from a starter she kept in the freezer. My grandfather swore it was from the original of like three hundred years ago or something." I'm watching and listening to Justin knowing he's on top of the poem and I'm waiting for him to make his turn. "Anyway, we used to eat pancakes and talk and I used to hear all about my family. Anyway, this poem is about how chiles are what glues his family together. Like when his grandmother dies and is gone forever, anytime he eats a chile it will bring her alive again. And he'll always feel connected." Bam! There's Justin nailed into the poem.

Sonia piped up again and now she feels back on the trail. She, who is Latina herself, begins to talk about culture and food and some of her views of politics in America and life in her ethnic community. After a half an hour of discussing the poem in class, this group hadn't even touched overtly on "critical" poetic elements like metaphor, lines, and stanzas. That was fine, we'd get there. Had they been knocked out, slowed down considerably? Most had, if not before class, at least by the end. We'd all had family bonding experiences over food, and this became the avenue by which people began to enter the poem. So, I've gone on a bit about this poem and a past discussion, but my point is this: If we search our own personal and human background and try to relate it to the poem we are reading, and we look carefully at the language the poet has used, most often we will be touched, knocked out, turned inside out without warning. It is the poet's job to write about life, about what it means to be human. And the hardest job of the writer is to make what is most private and unsensational to him, sensational to the reader.

Where Do Poems Come From?

Finding subject matter worthy enough for a poem can be one of the most difficult things a writer encounters. But this very notion of finding something "worthy" enough is problematic because the writer is saying that the poem deserves something better than he has come up with. This, unfortunately, is a losing battle in the search for good subject matter. So, how does a writer win? A poet finds subject matter that is moving, accessible, human. After all, people like to read about the world they live in, so writers write about it. So as readers, we need to attempt to see the world as a place filled with stories and poems. And if we don't, when a poet writes about these things, we may just miss the point of the poem or misunderstand the context in which the poet places the poem. There are poems hiding all around us—they are in corners of the room in spider webs, they are in the smooth handle of my grandfather's hammer in the garage, they are in the French toast for breakfast, and they are on the lawn of the old lady who lives across the street.

In an interview by Dave Smith, James Wright was asked about the subject matter for his poem "Lying in a Hammock at William Duffy's Farm in Pine Island, Minnesota," and he said that he was not trying to do anything heroic in that poem, but rather he was trying to capture a moment in his life where he felt a sense of delight. What he means by not being heroic is that the poem need not work on a grand level. It doesn't need to conquer us; it just needs to show us something and capture a moment. But in doing so, it is this type of poem that may move us, for these moments are often the smallest and most non-heroic moments, and for this reason they are also the most human. And often this type of poem forms itself into a short poem that is designed to express the thoughts, reflections, or feelings of the poet or persona, which is also known in poetry as a *lyric*. Sometimes as readers we may search too hard for the "great idea" only to have missed what the poem might be about. For instance, the last line of Mr. Wright's poem may be screaming out to be considered, but at the heart of the poem are all of these objects being noticed along the way to the last line. Over the years it may have been put into our heads that poems must be larger than life, must have something great to say. But poems are only great when they touch us, and when they tell us about our humanness and our histories. So, I often read and write by this principle: find a simple moment, a moment that is normal to me, what seems normal to the author, may be a quiet but striking image in the poem, and figure out what is important at the center of that. Let's take a look at the James Wright poem.

Lyric poem   is a short poem that is designed to express the thoughts, reflections or feelings of the poet or persona.

Lying in a Hammock at William Duffy's Farm in Pine Island, Minnesota
by James Wright

Over my head, I see the bronze butterfly
Asleep on the black trunk,
Blowing like a leaf in green shadow.
Down the ravine behind the empty house,
The cowbells follow one another
Into the distances of the afternoon.
To my right,
In a field of sunlight between two pines,
The droppings of last year's horses
Blaze up into golden stones.
I lean back, as the evening darkens and comes on.
A chicken hawk floats over, looking for home.
I have wasted my life.

Seeing the World as Poetic

So now that we've figured out how to find the poems, to know their hiding places—at least sometimes—we need to figure out how to make this a regular event. If we can do this in our own lives, then poetry is less daunting when we face it in a book because we know a little bit about how a poet is thinking. Consider this the reading process off the page. This is the part where we begin to put the process of reading into how we see everyday events. But to be able to do this we have to be open to redefining our world, to be ready to view it and define it at any moment and especially at the moment of reading.

Let's step back for a moment. If we go through the process of asking ourselves what we've noticed in the past two weeks that we haven't noticed before, what happens is that for one instant we stop or slow down long enough to see in our mind's eye a few new objects. And more, we slow ourselves long enough to let that thing take hold of us. So, if we apply this principle to reading a poem and slow ourselves, as well as being receptive to new subject matter, then we're likely to make some discovery along the way. Take, for example, a small child. He might go out to walk around the block. But how long does this take? When I walked with my son when he was two years old, a walk around the block might take forty minutes because every few yards he said "Look, Papa, a bug." Or "Look, Papa, a truck." The list of things he noticed was endless and most of them were rather exceptional findings, especially for him—he was two and some of these things he had never seen. But to define them in new ways, to watch the way a caterpillar moves is to see things as fresh. And to couple these with feelings, to put the concrete with the abstract, is to begin to realize poetry. So, I began to note these things on our walks around the block, and my, how many poems live on our block.

Let's spend a moment probing this idea of coupling concrete images with abstract thoughts or feelings. For instance, these words like tragic, harrowing, or sad mean little because they are **abstracts;** without **images** to represent them it is hard to relate to or attach to them. And, since poets create images regularly when they work with subject matter, as a reader we can look to images to hold some power in a poem. Concrete images allow abstracts to remain below the surface and thereby function as a subtle, implicit force in a poem. Hence, when reading we have to work with both the literal meanings and the range of possibilities behind those literal meanings. Take for instance the following image, the desire to hold someone. The image itself is concrete, but the emotion and the desire for connection is left below the surface of the image.

How I want to reach you;
slip my hands past your canvas
coat and hold you in the barn light as
night folds its dark clench over us.

Note that in this image, it is largely working based on its concrete parts. The two abstract notions come in the first and fourth lines. The first line gives us the sense that the lovers are apart, and there is longing and desire packed in the phrase "how I want." And in the fourth line there is a sense of near violence with the word "clench." But let's not apply that to the lovers because it's the night that has clenched them. So we might ask "Do they feel like there are forces at work against them, forces they're hiding from, forces that may drive them apart?" We don't know yet, but if we're asking these questions, we'd hope to see something happen around these ideas later in the poem.

As a reader, we want to remember that poems are representing the world to us. There are certainly thoughts and emotions in them and behind them. But there is no conspiracy against us by poets—they are not trying to confuse us. They aren't trying to set up a sea of words where we drown a slow and suffering death. Rather, they are attempting to capture some image and vision of the world where we will feel and think about our own and other's lives. They simply want us to see, and experience the world. Poets want us to walk with them, slowly, instead of speeding off on the freeway only to miss all that is whizzing by.

The Reader as the Hunted

I'm going to use a metaphor here for how we might view ourselves as a reader in relation to the poet. If we use hunting as a metaphor, the reader is the hunted. And when we read a poem and we stop and say, "Oh man, that's my life. Oh, I can't believe somebody else feels that way," we've been hit. By bullet, sling, or arrow, we've been brought down by the hunter. However, the poet—unlike the real hunter—isn't trying to kill us, but to stop us in our tracks, to catch us during a moment of grazing or perching, maybe even running (to and from work or school) and have us focus our life in a different direction. Most writers would tell us that the language of our daily life (advertising, radio, T.V., pop music, the newspaper) is utilitarian and usually in our capitalist society the language is there to get something out of us—money, a vote, or a piece of who we are. The poet's aim is to get us to stop for a moment and be absolutely stunned by our own life and see it in relation to the lives of others. So, we can come to the reading experience with the expectation that the writer is creating something for us that is an honest expression of language, of his experience, and an expression of the time in which they live or lived.

We ought to want to want this. I realize that's a bold a statement, one that brings back childhood memories of our mothers and fathers saying, "Eat your spinach, it's good for you." Our response was something like, "not on your life." And it's a reasonable response. If I tell a class, "you ought to like this poetry stuff," some think I'm out of my head. But let's remember that we've come to like broccoli, spinach, asparagus or chard. Poetry is rooted for us not in gimmicks or tricks—it's rooted in life. And when poets use that language which knocks us down when they present life to us, if we engage in the lives of others, hopefully it has taught us to live better.

Poetry is not utilitarian. But I'll say this about you applying poetry to your life in a seemingly utilitarian way. Students ask me all the time in classes how poetry will help them later. And I say something like this: Look, if you like poetry (at best) or at least have found a few poems you like and you understand the genre (at worst), here's how it works. Maybe you're a science major and you simply take to noticing things more, noticing the fine interconnectedness of things and you begin to see those relationships as somewhat poetic—a dance among cells. Maybe in your daily life it's simply noticing the people around us and how they act or react. Possibly we've slowed ourselves down enough to look closely at the system we're living in and its effects on us as people. Maybe in a tragic and horribly unfortunate situation we have a family member who is very ill and because we've read a poem about this we might be able to calculate something about how they're feeling and we're able to be someone solid for them. Maybe years from now we'll find poetry creeping up on us at very unexpected moments. And that may be utilitarian—but that's also at the core of living better, about our personal goals, about how we affect others, and ultimately reconciling with ourselves how we go about our daily business. To be in the eye of that storm—of poetry or daily living—is at the heart of our survivalist poetics.

To Experience

1. Think about something you've noticed in the past two weeks that you haven't noticed before. Then analyze its potential as a poetic subject. If you were to write a poem about this thing, would it be a good subject and why?
2. Look around your kitchen at some food objects—cereal, an apple, cookies, chips, broccoli, rice, pasta, tortillas, milk, beer, etc. Which one might make a good subject for a poem and why?

To Write

1. Choose a poem you've read, and write a short essay or journal entry discussing why the poem is an important poem to read, and make an argument for why it is, or will be, a lasting piece of literary art.

Chapter Two

How Readers Work, How Writers Work

Writers and readers usually come at poetry from two different angles. Writers struggle to capture their own world or a fictional world, as poetic, and relay an emotional or intellectual experience to the reader. And they do this using the craft of poetry the way a woodworker uses chisels, saws, dowels, and other tools and instruments of the trade. Poets are constantly looking at the world as a poetic place—a trip to a grocery store, a walk with the dog, or getting the kids out of the house and to school in the morning might all hold poems. So the poet sits down and attempts to articulate their world in an art form that will compound that experience emotionally or intellectually for the reader. One of the most difficult things a writer has to do is to make a poem mean something to the reader. We can assume that a poem will be transferring some emotional or intellectual

"As a writer, I'm the bird not the ornithologist."

Jim Harrison

weight to the reader. As a reader, this is important because then we can assume that there is some meaning to the subject matter or objects in that poem. And digging into the poem to decipher meaning is the requisite duty of the reader.

The quote by Jim Harrison, which begins this chapter, is an apt one for knowing the space we occupy as a reader and how we might approach things. When he states that "as a writer I'm the bird, not the ornithologist," Mr. Harrison tells us a great deal about how a writer works. When we sit back and watch birds, we see the birds simply going about their birdy business. They might be scouring seeds from the ground, filling their gullet with gravel, pulling worms or insects from the grass, possibly protecting a nest. That's just a bird's day. All of these actions are with purpose but are also simply a task in their day. Yet as the ornithologist we sit back and take note and then ask questions. Why are they eating that type of food? Why does a male grouse exhibit a certain wing flapping as a mating technique? Why, when the killdeer is in danger does it use a specific call? And who is the bird calling? And when we attempt to answer these questions, we look at many different factors: trends in the bird's behavior; changes in food availability during different seasons; common behavior among many killdeer during perceived danger (this is like looking at many poems by the same poet). And finally when we feel like we've pieced together enough pertinent details and information, we attempt a conclusion about the bird's behavior.

So, as a reader we are certainly analyzing a poem based on what we think is embedded in the words and why. We might look to other poems by the same author. We might use some knowledge of the writer's life. We may use some knowledge of history, politics, and social change. But we might also look to our own life at times and respond emotionally. There is a fine line between reading critically and analyzing poetry using our knowledge of poetics, an author's work, history, politics, economics, and psychology or simply responding to a poem from our own background. If we move too far into any of these areas, we may risk running far from a reasonable sense of the poem. So, what we hope is that when we read a poem and we use our poetic knowledge to pick at it, to dissect it, we reach a point where we are moved deeply by the experience in the poem. We ought to be touched enough that the evocative moments for the *persona* in the poem also become our own evocative moments.

Consider the following poem, "Oranges" by Gary Soto. Mr. Soto provides us with a reasonably ordinary experience—a boy and a girl meeting. What's more is that the emotional ingredient that comes forth from their meeting is one we've all felt and most likely even felt under the same circumstances as these two kids. The beauty of this poem is that one can know hardly anything technical about poetry and still take a great deal from it. We're on firm ground here; we're on familiar ground.

Oranges

by Gary Soto

The first time I talked
With a girl, I was twelve,
Cold, and weighted down
With two oranges in my jacket.
December. Frost cracking
Beneath my steps, my breath
Before me, then gone,
As I walked toward
Her house, the one whose
Porch light burned yellow
Night and day, in any weather.
A dog barked at me, until
she came out pulling
At her gloves, face bright
With rouge. I smiled,
Touched her shoulder, and led
Her down the street, across
A used car lot and a line
Of newly planted tress,
Until we were breathing
Before a drugstore. We
Entered, the tiny bell
Bringing the saleslady
Down a narrow aisle of goods.
I turned to the candies
Tiered like bleachers
And asked what she wanted—
Light in her eyes, a smile
Starting at the corners
Of her mouth. I fingered
A nickel in my pocket,
And when she lifted a chocolate
That cost a dime,
I didn't say anything.
I took the nickel from
My pocket, then an orange,
And set them quietly on
The counter. When I looked up,
The lady's eyes met mine,
And held them, knowing
Very well what it was all

> About
>   Outside,
> A few cars hissing past,
> Fog hanging like old
> Coats between the trees.
> I took my girl's hand
> In mine for two blocks,
> Then released it to let
> Her unwrap the chocolate
> That was so bright against
> The gray of December
> That, from some distance,
> Someone might have thought
> I was making a fire in my hands.

Once we've managed to take some meaning from the poem, we might ask a few questions about it. Here are some questions you could ask, generally, of just about any poem, and you can tailor them to the specific poem you're reading: 1) What happens intellectually/ emotionally/ psychologically to the *persona* (the speaker) or main character during the poem? 2) Is there a central object or metaphor in the poem that seems important to the overall meaning or your interpretation? And 3) how does the poem end and why does it end this way? We might tailor these for the poem "Oranges" to ask, what effect does the adult have on the boy and how does the boy feel (and why) by the end of the poem? Why is the poem titled "Oranges"? What role do they play? And finally, why does Mr. Soto introduce the adult toward the end of the poem? These questions will help us get at the core of the poem through the means of poetic elements, but will also allow us to dig into the emotional experience of the poem and the connection we have to it.

My Interpretation vs. What I'm Told the Poem Means

One of the hardest things about poetry is that somewhere along the line in our growing up, someone told us we didn't have the keys to the poetry door—that only they or the poet or other academics had the key. So, very often I hear people say, "Man, I just don't get poetry." People will ask me at a party, "So what do you do?" When I tell them I teach poetry and that I'm also a poet, they usually say something like, "I liked poetry once, but it always seems so far out there—and I never really got it." But that feeling didn't develop on its own. What's likely is that the feeling developed because a teacher told this person that they didn't "get it." Therefore the "meaning" of a poem they heard in class seemed abstract and foreign, unrelated to their own thought process. This is common and it certainly accounts for a hunk of the population feeling as if they don't understand poetry. Just as troubling though, and at the other end of the spectrum, is the reader of poetry who feels as if a poem can mean anything they want it to mean just because it's a poem. There is a middle ground between these two.

Beyond the teacher who has told us that we don't "get it," another force at work against our understanding poetry is our comfort with the language of poetry. When we read novels or essays, for the most part all prose, we feel a greater comfort. And we feel an ease in that writing because largely we all do it—for school, for work, for writing letters. It's here that we begin to feel the disconnect with poetry. We don't all regularly engage in the language of poetry. We don't all necessarily view our own lives as poetic adventures. So, often there is not an immediate sense of connection within poetry because the structure on the page is different than prose. The syntax (word order) may be different than prose, and some other elements of language use (metaphor, symbolism, line structure) may be different than prose. But if we begin to gather a sense of what's coming, rather than looking up the poetic tracks and seeing a barreling locomotive coming at us, we can get on board and go for a comfortable, first-class trip.

The great beauty of combating these two forces—language and our past experiences with poetry—is that we can become a sharper reader, able to have reactions to the language at moments we expect and at moments we don't. And the end result is that as much as we read a poem, the poem reads us. The embedded intelligence of a poem, the meaning of these words someone has written before us, comes to mean something in our life. But not just because we react to them; rather the words are directing us toward a feeling or a thought, and we're meeting them in a poetic space, which has caused others similar reactions. We fit into the humanity of the poem, the history of the work, some piece of the writer's life previous to our coming to know it. And it is for this reason that when we sit around and discuss poetry, we feel a part of something larger than ourselves.

In the following poem, note the words and phrases that might strike you, create tension, cause resolution in your emotional response to the poem. And too, note what words might cause you to relate to something written by a poet who lived during the T'ang Dynasty from 618–905 A.D.

Cups of Jade
by Huang Pien

Where the lotus pool
Is fragrant with its flowers,
We drank our last farewell
From cups of jade.

You thought I shunned you
When I, quickly turning,

Hid my face from you,
And would not look again.

Ah!
But being man,
How could you know, beloved,
That it was to wipe
The scalding tears away?

While this poem comes from the long past Chinese poetic tradition, note how the subject matter still clings to our contemporary life. I'm struck when I read this poem by this idea of the misunderstanding—that one lover thinks the other is shunning when in fact it is out of sadness that she turns to hide the tears. In that line about the tears, the word "scalding" is the one which seems to bring the most to me. It drills into my own heart the sense of sadness at the parting, how passionate and painful the tears are. And it is here in the poem where, as I may be reading from my own experienced relative events, I am also being led to those events by what the poem has to offer. So, there is a payoff for me here by being able to straddle the line between finding my own world in this poem and yet allowing the language to lead me to knew discoveries wherein the author creates for us all, a new place to find ourselves.

Knowing the Writer's Tools

As readers, we need to work with some of the same tools as writers. We need to understand how a writer might use *metaphor and simile.* We must know something about *lines and stanzas.* We will certainly be helped by understanding something about *rhyme and meter and rhythm.* And let us never forget the *persona* in a poem, that person who "tells" the poem or what the poem is about—we need to know something about them. Let's not forget Mr. Harrison's quote at the beginning of this chapter about the bird and the ornithologist. If we come to know these elements of poetics and some techniques a writer uses, we have not become the bird. We have become a knowledgeable and intelligent ornithologist.

If we know that we might link the meaning of words from line to line, that we should inspect closely what change(s) the persona is going through, that we ought to notice any symbols and important images, then we are on the road to finding some meaning in a poem. Something we might remember is that every poem may not have a distinct point. In some poems, it is easy to find a point—the author may have decided from the first moment sitting down that he would head toward a given line or a given meaning in the poem. But in other cases the long walk toward discovery has yielded many things—much beautiful language, a music in the poem, fine images, many small movements of our hearts and minds along the way—but no one distinct point at the end. Take the following poem, "Axe Handles" by Gary Snyder. By the end of the poem, it's clear that Mr. Snyder is giving us a point to consider.

Axe Handles

by Gary Snyder

One afternoon the last week in April
Showing Kai how to throw a hatchet
One-half turn and it sticks in a stump.
He recalls the hatchet-head
Without a handle, in the shop
And go gets it, and wants it for his own.
A broken-off axe handle behind the door
Is long enough for a hatchet,
We cut it to length and take it
With the hatchet head
And working hatchet, to the wood block.
There I begin to shape the old handle
With the hatchet, and the phrase
First learned from Ezra Pound
Rings in my ears!
"When making an axe handle
            the pattern is not far off."
And I say this to Kai
"Look: We'll shape the handle
By checking the handle
Of the axe we cut with—"
And he sees. And I hear it again:
It is in Lu Ji's *Wen Fu,* fourth century
A.D. "Essay on Literature"—in the
Preface: "In making the handle
Of an axe
By cutting wood with an axe
The model is indeed near at hand."
My teacher Shih-hsiang Chen
Translated that and taught it years ago
And I see: Pound was an axe,
Chen was an axe, I am an axe
And my son a handle, soon
To be shaping again, model
And tool, craft of culture,
How we go on.

We are able to follow this poem through with relative ease, maybe because of the narrative thread in the poem, and we finally arrive at this point about crafting culture, generations, family, teachers, and our own teaching. But in other poems we might not be held by a narrative thread. In fact, the author may work against the idea entirely. In this next poem, "March Walk" by Jim Harrison, note how we amble along in the poem shifting, floating from one image to another, and one idea to another. He is literally taking us on a walk.

March Walk

by Jim Harrison

I was walking because I wasn't upstairs sitting.
I could have been looking for pre-1900 gold coins
in the woods all afternoon. What a way to make a living!
The same mastodon was there only three hundred years from
where I last saw him. I felt the sabers on the saber tooth,
the hot wet breath on the back of my hand. Three deer
and a number of crows, how many will remain undisclosed:
It wasn't six and it wasn't thirty. There were four girls
ranging back to 1957. The one before that just arrived
upstairs. There was that long morose trip into the world
hanging onto my skin for a quarter of a mile, shed with some
difficulty. There was one dog, my own, and one grouse
not my own. A strong wind flowed through us like
dry water. I kissed a scar on a hip. I found a rotting
crab apple and a distant relative to quartz. You could spend
a lifetime and still not walk to an island. I met none of the
dead today having released them yesterday at three o'clock.
If you're going to make love to a woman you have to give
her some of your heart. Else don't. If I had found a gold coin
I might have left it there with my intermittent interest in
money. The dead snipe wasn't in the same place but the rocks
were. The apple tree was a good place to stand. Every late fall
the deer come there for dessert. They will stand there for days
waiting for a single apple to tumble from the upmost limb.

Now that you've read Mr. Harrison's poem, go back and read it again. This is a poem that warrants a few reads. We might initially be inclined to dismiss it as loose, as out-there-on-the-edge, as entirely incoherent. But maybe that's because we're trying too hard to find a point. Maybe we're trying to make a point. If we look at how carefully the language is crafted, we'll begin to note he is indeed taking us on an intellectual, physical, psychological, and historical walk. If there's any point to be made it might simply be that the poet has taken us on a walk, a time when we physically wander, amble, stride along and often our mind and heart do the same thing—they wander while we wander. And this poem may remind us that we associate our past with physical places and things in the world. And at an even larger level we might read this poem as one which places us into the continuity of history, into the continuity of the natural world.

Ambiguity and Owning My Own Perspective

Ambiguity   in poetry is when a word, group of words or line(s) has more than one meaning.

Ambiguity   in poetry is when a word, group of words or line(s) has more than one meaning. And this may be the sole factor that has poetry seeming so hard to decipher. Because poets work with compressed language, they rely on ambiguity to squeeze much meaning from their word choices. So when a poet creates multiple meanings from a word, they will often link some of those meanings at later points in the poem. And then the words in a poem become braided together and most strands of the braid (words of the poem) are woven, but some strands are left dangling just around the edge of the braid in all their luster.

Let's finish by tackling this notion of what you think versus what someone might tell you a poem means. First it's important to come to some sense of meaning when reading a poem—otherwise why read at all. Part of that lies in confidence, knowing you can come to some conclusion about a poem—point or no point—and knowing why you came to that conclusion. That begins with looking at language closely. It also means not placing extreme personal value judgments on the poem. And it means that you are willing to meet the author on their terms sometimes—that after having a personal response, you look at what the poet might have been intending by looking at lines, images, word choice, rhyme, and rhythm. And then we're all close to the same place, the same forest of lines and words, bird and ornithologist, and we're headed toward clear identification and a jaw-dropping gape at the wonder of a moment.

To Experience

1. Choose another poem from the book—or outside, maybe one of your favorites—and apply one of the following questions to it:
   a) What happens intellectually/ emotionally/ psychologically to the *persona* (the speaker) or main character during the poem?
   b) Is there a central object or metaphor in the poem that seems important to the overall meaning or your interpretation?

2. After reading a poem from this chapter or another, ask yourself what you think the poem means to you. Once you've answered that question, wade through the poem finding words related to the meaning you've come up with—do the words and their sum meanings and relationships equal some sense of what you've decided the poem means?

To Write

1. Choose a poem to read, and then write a short essay or journal entry discussing how you thought your way through the poem.
2. Choose a poem from the chapter and write a short essay or journal entry discussing how the persona changes or evolves during the poem. You might also discuss what specific words and lines lead you to your discovery.

Chapter Three

Literary Criticism:

Critical Approaches to Meeting a Poem

When reading poetry, there are many ways we might meet a poem on the page. And often, as already discussed, we will first wade through the language reacting and responding from a very human level. We might attempt to make sense of the language, to discover what function the poetic elements serve, to uncover a point behind the poem we believe the author is providing. These are valid ways to understand what is in front of us, and they are certainly at the root of analyzing literature. However, there are academic schools of thought in the field of literature called literary criticism. Literary criticism is a discipline concerned with the range of enquiries about literature—criticism pursues such root questions as what literature is, what it does, and what the worth of literature is.

This chapter deals mostly with general outlines of the more prominent twentieth century critical theories. Though Western critical theory has been in place since the fourth century B.C., and has had a range of movements

"It is a great river of possibilities, language, swirling around us all the time—people talk to each other. They come upon swoops of realization and vistas—even the syllables have meanings."

William Stafford

since, the twentieth century proved a time of radical reappraising of traditional theoretical approaches to literature. And while there are a number of theories and models not represented in this chapter, those which appear here ought to give a variety of perspectives and critical approaches for many types of poems. In applying them to your reading, you may find that there are some poems crying out for the application of a specific theory. Take for example Linda Pastan's poem "Marks" which we may find fitting well with a Feminist Theory reading. On the other hand, there might be poems which are more subtly approached and may have various possibilities as to what theoretical consideration you would give them. But before we tackle these more contemporary approaches let's scan a bit of history behind critical theory first.

The Western tradition of literary theory is rooted in Plato's writings from the fourth century B.C. In his *Republic,* Plato indicted poets on two counts: that they simply imitated what they observed and that the art appealed to the worst in human nature. But a generation after Plato these claims were countered by Aristotle in his work titled, *Poetics.* In this he developed a set of principles for literary composition which have been of lasting importance in the Western tradition of literature. These "rules" functioned around the notion that time, action, and place were the three unifying forces in a literary work. And the Aristotelian approach was largely observed until nearly the end of the seventeenth century.

The Renaissance proved a time of some shift in literary approach and one of the more notable and well-known works is *The Defence of Poesie* written at the end of the sixteenth century by Sir Philip Sidney. While much of the literary thought of that era focused on the moral worth of literature and the relationship of literature to reality, Sidney added to this a concept still in practice today: that it is the responsibility of poetry (of all literature) to present moral and philosophical arguments and truths in a manner which pulls them from the abstract and makes them immediately concrete for the reader. While this notion has remained for some time, nearly a century after Sidney's assertion John Dryden claimed that the primary concern of literature should be to offer delight and instruction through an accurate representation of the world. This is (and was) often taken to mean art for the sake of entertainment that instructs. This idea remained at the core of literary thought through the eighteenth century. And as a residual effect, by viewing the art and cultural practices of the time, it is evident that the aristocracy of Europe especially believed in this idea.

The nineteenth century brought great change as the Romantics were furiously shifting from what they viewed as a constrictive and narrow path of the previous century. Among many, William Wordsworth was a ground-breaking poet advocating in favor of ethos. He believed that the poet is a speaker whose feelings and expressions are to be seen as "carried alive into the heart by passion." This notion linked directly to the Aristotelian idea, and it also rubbed against principles from the near centuries that art was concerned with the moral quandaries of the time, which largely translated to religious dilemmas. Later in the nineteenth century, we see the development of other core ideas revolving around culture and the role of art. The aesthetic theory developing at this time was the art for art's sake principle. And the poet and theorist Matthew Arnold believed that poetics (indeed art altogether) should take over the cultural and moral role that religion had played in previous centuries. Indeed this was a dramatic shift that sent the artistic and theoretic worlds into prolific change throughout the twentieth century.

We have witnessed in our recent past century theorists building on all of this past thinking and reevaluating some of its usefulness. While much of the early twentieth century literary theory revolved around the Russian Formalists from the 1920's, theorists in the later part of the century began to call into question the importance of "the author" as connected to the text's meaning. These theorists believed that meaning was not derived from what the author intended to say, the author's past, or the social/historical conditions from which the author came. Rather the meaning of a text was generated by language and culture.

Now that we've reached the twentieth century, the following critical theories will provide you some critical approaches from our near past. The following outlines of theories may help your understanding of poems, further your discussions, or provide you with an analytical framework with which you may write about a poem. It's important to remember that while applying the critical approaches, what the author has written (what you think you see as the author's point) may not agree with what the "critic" observes and concludes.

Some Schools of Thought

Archetypal Theory

This literary theory is primarily concerned with discovering how the major themes or motifs in a poem (or other literary work) are related to recurring patterns of characters, images, and narratives. This theory is based on the notion that images and narratives are structured and only important according to their connections to archetypal models throughout human history. These characters, images, and narrative structures would be identifiably relative to archetypes from a variety of dreams, myths, and modes of social behavior.

Deconstruction

This method of analysis assumes that language refers to and is connected only to itself rather than any reality outside the text. The text is therefore related to the social, cultural, and political use and implications of the language which may indeed raise multiple conflicting interpretations. However, these interpretations supercede any author intent perceived by the reader. Deconstruction takes apart the standard logic of language which authors use to make claims and structure a work. Hence, Deconstruction sets out to illustrate how text will subvert itself because there are nuances of positions opposite to the position that the author and text set out to uphold or solve. Finally, Deconstruction demonstrates that every text generates innumerable contradictory and indeterminate meanings.

Feminist Theory

Feminist theory examines the ways in which literature has been shaped according to gender. This theoretical approach explores privilege based on sexual difference in the form and content, production, reception, analysis, and evaluation of literature. Three core principles applied to the Feminist approach are: 1) that the Western world has been a patriarchal culture and subjugates women to men in the majority of cultural roles; 2) while sex is determined by anatomy, gender is defined socially (masculine gender has historically been ascribed the dominant features that cultures find socially valuable while the feminine has been ascribed passive, acquiescent features Western culture derides); and 3) patriarchal ideology pervades the literary canon and has largely been written by men for men and the analysis and critiques of such work are filled with masculine assumptions, interests, and reasoning. Hence, a resultant factor of Feminist theory has been a move to identify female subject matter, the exploration and discovery of a female world literary history, and distinguishing a female/feminine experience.

Formalism

Formalist theory flourished in the 1920's from a Russian school of literary theorists. The Formalists viewed literature by paying close attention to the style, arrangement, or the artistic approach. These theorists de-emphasized content and analyzed the text itself relative to formal aspects of a literary work, feeling it was important to view the text as separate from biographical, social, political, or psychological contexts.

The Geneva School (Phenomenology Theory)

This group of theorists popularized their work in the 1930's. They believed that a literary work exposed the personality of an author and this was a reason to read literature. Because writing is an intentional act, directed by the author, by reading the entire body of work by an author it is possible to reach a conclusion about the writer's vision of him/herself and the world. They were likely to focus on attitudes of the author, obsessions shown in the writing, and political notions arising in a body of work.

Marxist Theory

Marxist criticism typically explains a literary work by viewing it in the context of its historical time. Therefore, the poem (play, novel, or story) is not viewed as a timeless piece of literature. Rather, the reader needs to closely analyze the economic, political, and religious ideology of that specific time and place. In applying Marxist theory, it is important to view the positions and interests of particular classes and how they work as typically competing forces in a literary work. For example, the reader might analyze how characters from the dominant social and economic class might further their interests over the working class.

New Historicism

Influenced by Marxist theory, New Historicism approaches literature as representative of a historical and cultural setting. When applying New Historicism, the reader must analyze the historical, social, and cultural implications of a literary work and then extend the analysis to the historical period in which the work was produced. Therefore, the critic analyzes literature as interacting with history, not as simply a product of a given time, and the point of reading literature is to uncover the ideology of that historical period.

Psychoanalytic/Psychological Theory

This theoretical school is largely based on Freud's model of the ego, superego, and is as well as theory about authors and artists being sophisticated beings able to control sexual desires for such a higher goal as art. Hence, this criticism analyzes: 1) a piece of literature in the context of the author's psychological conflicts; 2) a reader's responses to literature; and 3) it may make assumptions of the psychological life of an author by viewing unconscious revelations in the writing. This theory also includes work by Carl Jung's archetypal theory that in the human unconscious we possess a collective body of archetypal models. Therefore, a reader might analyze a piece of literature viewing how an author or character responds to an archetypal human situation.

Reader-Response Theory

This school of literary criticism believes that individual readers re-create the text and each person may read something varied in its meaning based on his/her own experience. Therefore, the Reader-Response critic is engaged in an analysis of the reader/author relationship, discerning ambiguities, the reader's role in filling in gaps the author may have left, creating a set of assumptions in order to navigate the poem, and the reader's inferences he/she creates in order to understand the work. Because the author has put incentives to the reader's responses and limitations to the work, some analyses may be rejected.

Structuralism

This school of literary thought was based on the idea that language and culture are both structures that can be analyzed and understood by viewing their systems of signs and symbols. Therefore, the structuralist critic analyzes a piece of literature as a series of interlocking signs (linguistic and cultural) which fit together as a piece of the larger set of rules that governs all literature. Structuralists will consider all of the areas of the humanities as "structures" to consider in their analysis (i.e. anthropology, sociology, politics, religion, etc.) and by gaining access from these various fields, the significance of a poem may be obtained.

Of course, the theories of literary criticism mentioned here are not all the schools of thought but a sampling of the many critical theories that burgeoned in the twentieth century. You might find yourself gravitating to one of these theories that suits your manner of thinking and suits your sense of approaching poetry. You may find that for the sense of sitting on your couch and enjoying a poem one afternoon (maybe you're flipping through an anthology for pleasure), the last thing you want to do is to apply academic, critical theory; rather, you want to place the poem into your own life and simply enjoy the language. However, when engaging in group discussions about poetry and for writing papers about poems, you'll probably wish to engage in a more critical discussion that analyzes the poem from one of various angles. For a bit of initial practice, read the following poems and apply a critical theory to each of them creating an interpretation based in critical theory.

Marks

by Linda Pastan

My husband gives me an A
for last night's supper,
an incomplete for my ironing,
a B plus in bed.
My son says I'm average,
an average mother, but if
I put my mind to it
I could improve.
My daughter believes
in Pass/Fail and tells me
I pass. Wait 'til they learn
I'm dropping out.

What Work Is

by Philip Levine

We stand in the rain in a long line
waiting at Ford Highland Park. For work.
You know what work is—if you're
old enough to read this you know what
work is, although you may not do it.
Forget you. This is about waiting,
shifting from one foot to another.
Feeling the light rain falling like mist
into your hair, blurring your vision
until you think you see your own brother
ahead of you, maybe ten places.
You rub your glasses with your fingers,
and of course it's someone else's brother,
narrower across the shoulders than
yours but with the same sad slouch, the grin
that does not hide the stubbornness,
the sad refusal to give in to
rain, to the hours wasted waiting,
to the knowledge that somewhere ahead
a man is waiting who will say, "No,
we're not hiring today," for any
reason he wants. You love your brother,
now suddenly you can hardly stand
the love flooding you for your brother,
who's not beside you or behind or
ahead because he's home trying to
sleep off a miserable night shift
at Cadillac so he can get up
before noon to study his German.
Works eight hours a night so he can sing
Wagner, the opera you hate most,
the worst music ever invented.
How long has it been since you told him
you loved him, held his wide shoulders,
opened your eyes wide and said those words,
and maybe kissed his cheek? You've never
done something so simple, so obvious,
not because you're too young or too dumb,
not because you're jealous or even mean
or incapable of crying in

the presence of another man, no,
just because you don't know what work is.

Blink Your Eyes

by Sekou Sundiata

(Remembering Sterling A. Brown)

I was on my way to see my woman
but the Law said I was on my way
thru a red light red light red light
and if you saw my woman
you could understand,
I was just being a man.
It wasn't about no light
it was about my ride
and if you saw my ride
you could dig that too, you dig?
Sunroof stereo radio black leather
bucket seats sit low you know,
the body's cool but the tires are worn.
Ride when the hard times come, ride
when they're gone, in other words
the light was green.

I could wake up in the morning
without a warning
and my world could change;
blink your eyes.
All depends, all depends on the skin,
all depends on the skin you're living in.

Up to the window comes the Law
with his hand on his gun
what's up? What's happening?
I said I guess
that's when I really broke the law.
He said *a routine, step out the car*
a routine, *assume the position.*
Put your hands up in the air
you know the routine, like you just don't care.
License and registration.
Deep was the night and the light
from the North star on the car door, déjà vu
we've been through this before,
why did you stop me?

Somebody has to stop you.
I watch the news, you always lose.
You're unreliable, that's undeniable.
This is serious, you could be dangerous.

I could wake up in the morning
without a warning
and my world could change;
blink your eyes.
All depends, all depends on the skin,
all depends on the skin you're living in.

New York City, they got laws
can't no bruthas drive outdoors,
in certain neighborhoods, on particular streets
near and around certain types of people.
They got laws.
All depends, all depends on the skin,
all depends on the skin you're living in.

Poem for the Young White Man Who Asked Me How I, an Intelligent Well-Read Person, Could Believe in the War between Races

by Lorna Dee Cervantes

In my land there are no distinctions.
The barbed wire politics of oppression
have been torn down long ago. The only reminder
of past battles, lost or won, is a slight
rutting of the fertile fields.

In my land
people write poems about love,
full of nothing but contented childlike syllables.
Everyone reads Russian short stories and weeps.
There are no boundaries.
There is no hunger, no
complicated famine or greed.

I am not a revolutionary.
I don't even like political poems.
Do you think I can believe in a war between races?
I can deny it. I can forget about it
when I'm safe,
living on my own continent of harmony
and home, but I am not
there.

I believe in revolution
because everywhere the crosses are burning,
sharp-shooting goose-steppers round every corner,
there are snipers in the schools. . .
(I know you don't believe this.
You think this is nothing
but faddish exaggeration. But they
are not shooting at you.)

I'm marked by the color of my skin.
The bullets are discrete and designed to kill slowly.
They are aiming at my children.
These are facts.
Let me show you my wounds: my stumbling mind, my
"excuse me" tongue, and this
nagging preoccupation
with the feeling of not being good enough.

These bullets bury deeper than logic.
Racism is not intellectual.
I can not reason these scars away.

Outside my door
there is a real enemy
who hates me.

I am a poet
who yearns to dance on rooftops,
to whisper delicate lines about joy
and the blessings of human understanding.
I try. I go to my land, my tower of words and
bolt the door, but the typewriter doesn't fade out
the sounds of blasting and muffled outrage.
My own days bring me slaps on the face.
Every day I am deluged with reminders
that this is not
my land

and this is my land.

I do not believe in the war between races

but in this country
there is a war.

To Experience

1. Choose a poem of your liking that you believe might be open to more than one interpretation. Then offer two analyses of the same poem.

To Write

1. Apply a literary theory to one of the poems at the end of this chapter and write a short critique of the work within the model of the theory. For example you may choose to write a Feminist critique of Linda Pastan's poem "Marks." Or you may wish to look at Phillip Levine's poem "What Work Is" and offer a Marxist critique.

.

Chapter Four

How a Poem Is Built:

Metaphor, Symbol, and Point of View

Writers work in many different ways. When talking with other writers about how we work, it's always striking to me how different the answers are. But, there is one common practice at the core of a poet's work, and that is the act of discovery while writing. During a conversation with poet, Albert Garcia (author of "School's Ugliest Girl Dies"), he said to me that he never knows where he's going in a poem, that it's often a surprise to him when he finds out. My response to him was that the whole idea scared me. I like to know where I'm headed. Yet, after talking more, we realized that I engage in this same sense of not knowing entirely where I'm headed. And, much the way a person might spend a day along a river, a poet approaches a poem.

"Sometimes I feel that I am just an audience for words floating by and through. But the possibilities seem inexhaustible: I don't know what story will rise up out of that deep well of experience, and I'm always fascinated by how there's something there to work with every morning."

Naomi Shihab Nye

She is at the river. She has a trail, a bike path, or some place to walk. She decides on a general direction—upstream or down. And then she sets out. It may be a long walk; it may be a short walk. But many times the poet/walker doesn't know this until she's already walking and suddenly she breaks through some bushes and there, swimming, is a small otter ferrying twigs and leaves. She watches for a short while. Then she decides to walk on, and, of course, she's stopped short again—this time by a doe and her young fawn. Soon, having not gone as far as she wished, the poet looks at her watch and decides that it's time to head back. She enjoyed the walk. She saw some great things. She is thrilled to have seen an otter, an animal she has never before seen in the wild. There is fulfillment. Then she says, "Maybe next time we'll get further."

This is much the same for writing poems. The poet begins writing with a general sense of where she's headed—at best a sense of an idea but maybe just a sense of language, of words. Like the walk, she knows a bit about the landscape and something that has caused us to walk in the first place. But implied in the statement about getting further is the notion that somehow she didn't reach her destination. That is the difference between hiking and poetry. The poet will consider her destination reached once she decides to turn around. The next walk will be a different poem

While writing, poets are often in the act of discovering. They have most likely not gone into things with a clear map. And, if they did, sometimes the journey changes. So this means that writers are regularly in the act of discovery. As the Nobel Laureate Seamus Heaney states, "We are in the act of revealing the self to the self, revealing some sense of our self within our cultures". This revealing one's self and the act of capturing the right words to express it, this creation of the world for others, is the act of discovery for any writer. This means that as readers we too will discover. We will retrace the steps of the writer's walk along the river and find the otter, the doe, and the fawn, some moment of their life—and very importantly ours—which becomes revealed, having come clean from beneath layers and layers of silt washed up on the banks of our lives. And when we notice a piece of our own life in a poem, we can place ourselves in the cultural, social, or historical context that the poet is writing about. Then we are connected to the poet's reality and a broad human experience which helps create culture and literature.

Imagery: Metaphor, Simile, and Symbols

When writers sit down to work, they approach writing a poem much the same way a woodworker might approach the workshop or the way a chef might approach coming into a kitchen. In these cases, the person walking into the room has something to work with but needs to mold it. The writer has paper and a pen. The woodworker has wood and tools. The chef has ingredients and kitchen appliances. But most importantly, what each has is a set of conceptual tools—the elements of the craft. The woodworker knows that a certain type and grain of wood will sand and stain best; he knows that a certain style leg will support a table best. The chef knows that a wine-based sauce is different than a butter-based sauce; she knows that grilling might be right for a steak and poaching is right for salmon. Without belaboring the point, the writer too knows that there are methods and elements on which she needs to rely in order to make the poem a poem, the elements that will distinguish a poem from a story, essay, or play, and elements that will best shape the experience she is writing about.

When we read prose, we are usually taken by the trajectory of the narrative or ideas. We enjoy good solid writing—writing which employs rhythm, imagery, and development of characters or ideas. And poets do employ some of these things, namely rhythm and imagery. But how? Well, when we look at a poem, we know enough to say something like, "It has short lines so it must be a poem." Or maybe we read a bit and we say "It's a poem because it rhymes." And that's good. We are intuitively noting what we believe makes a poem. And we're right on both counts. As we read poems that we refer to as literary poetry—poetry which works to capture the human experience and does not place its commercial use as top priority—we need to note that writers will use elements such as imagery, metaphor, simile, rhyme, meter, lines, and stanzas to create a desired effect in the poem and inevitably on the reader. In this chapter, we'll look at imagery and point of view as key components to the structure of a poem.

Imagery

Writers strive to arrest the reader, to hold us in a moment. This is no easy task, but when writers do it, and when they do it well, they achieve something powerful. But, how do writers do this? One of the ways this is accomplished in poetry is through *imagery*. Put simply, an *image* is a representation of objects, feelings, or ideas either literally or figuratively. And through imagery, writers turn *abstracts*—feelings and ideas—into part of our physical, concrete world. Most often when we speak of images, we mean that we can see something. But, don't forget that generally we use the term *image* when we discuss those

Imagery   is a concrete representation of objects, feelings, or ideas using either literal or figurative language associated with our senses.

Image   is a representation of objects feelings, or ideas either literal or figuratively.

Abstracts   are feelings and ideas into part of our physical, concrete world.

words that touch our other senses too. The poet, Virgil used the term *imago*, which meant that a place or object described had an entire sense about it that was not just physical but emotional and/or intellectual. When images are used in poems, they give the reader a heightened perception of the world, they work on the reader's senses, and the writer's world begins to become part of ours.

Often in poetry, there is more to an image than meets the eye. Under or behind it there is a feeling or an idea being expressed. This may simply be one feeling or idea attached to the image. Or, the feeling may rise from the *context* of the poem—a sense of what's happening, where we're going in a poem. But images should stand in front of abstract feelings and thoughts and veil them. And when this happens, writers create provocative images which show us something rather than tell. This is when language begins to take on power and become something much more than mere reporting. If we want reporting, we can subscribe to our local paper. But when we want to be swept away in the poem, we need language that turns in on us, which takes our sight, our ears, our heart.

Context   is an overall sense of what's happening in a poem, what meaning or forces are being constructed in either the whole poem or part of a poem.

Simile and Metaphor

Images can be created in a number of different ways, but no matter how writers create them or what type of image they create, in poetry, images are our guides. As a young writer, I once had an instructor/mentor of mine say two things to me that have hung around as two of the best basic pieces of advice I may have ever been told. First he told me, "It is too much to ask of a reader to give them abstracts in the first sentence of a poem—give them images." And he told me (however harsh it was at the time, it held on as good advice), "I don't really care if you tell me how you feel in the poem—show me something and I'll figure out what I'm supposed to feel." As a writer, crafting good images builds a stronger poem because the images do the work for me. So, as a reader of poems, I know I can look to the images as a spring from which emotional or intellectual forces will flow. Hence the reader must always be aware that the details of a poem, these images are doing some work, allowing some piece of the poem to unfold. When we notice these moments in a poem, we need to read beneath the words and ask what is implied, what can we infer from all the various levels the language is working on.

One of the ways writers create vibrant images in a poem is to use *similes and metaphors*. These types of images are based on comparisons and relay an abstract idea to the reader in very concrete terms. As readers, we know them and we use them regularly in our daily speech without consciously thinking about it. A *simile* is a comparison using the words *like* or *as*. For

Simile   is a comparison of two things using the words *like* or *as*.

example, "The brown, winter river moved *like* molasses." Or, "The horse's flanks were strong *as* alder." In the first example, we have details—brown and winter—to give us color and a sense of temperature, depth, season. But when the writer uses "*like* molasses," we now know more about how the river is moving and what the color really is. In the case of the horse, we can draw some conclusions about how strong the horse is or what his flanks might feel like. Alder is a hard and strong wood; hence, the author has chosen this detail carefully and appropriately. What's more, it's a natural detail that might also lend a hand in describing the horse's setting or extending the horse into the setting. Notice in the simile, unlike the metaphor, the horse remains a horse and the river remains the river, but the comparison still serves to add depth and information to the image. Take a look at the following poem by Langston Hughes in which similes are used to guide how we think and feel in the poem.

Harlem (A Dream Deferred)

by Langston Hughes

What happens to a dream deferred?

> Does it dry up
> Like a raisin in the sun?
> Or fester like a sore—
> And then run?
> Does it stink like rotten meat?
> Or crust and sugar over—
> Like a syrupy sweet?
>
> Maybe it just sags
> Like a heavy load.

Or does it Explode?

A *metaphor* is a comparison that says one thing *is* another. For example, I might turn to my friend and say "Luis *is* the moon." This is a very basic metaphor, but it serves the purpose for the moment. The thing to remember in this example is that now Luis is no longer Luis; rather, he has taken on the qualities of the moon. The effect is that the metaphor now causes the reader to know something about the image more than its concrete details, to think about Luis having the qualities of the moon ascribed to him, and ultimately we are pushed to a deeper level in the poem. And note that the metaphor

Metaphor   is a direct comparison of two concrete objects in which one object takes on the characteristic of the other.

works as a comparison of two concrete objects. Therefore, the writer doesn't tell us the abstract nature of Luis—he simply takes on the implicit qualities of the moon. The metaphor can take us to a deeper level by intensifying the abstract meaning of physical symbols in the poem, developing the persona of the poem, and/or allowing themes to emerge.

Metaphors can function at various levels in a poem. At times, they function within the line or a small number of lines. Maybe a metaphor serves to power a stanza and is the overriding image. Aside from the standard metaphor, there are two types of metaphors commonly used: the *implied metaphor* and the *extended* or *controlling metaphor*. The *implied metaphor* does not actually state in the comparison what our main object is being compared to; rather, it implies the comparison usually through action or ascribing attributes. For example, we compare this man to a fish by saying, *he finned his way across the room/eyeing the bait.* Or, in the following image the implication applies to both people: *Mother squawked at me as I fluttered out the back door.* These metaphors work on a very subtle level but their impact should not be taken lightly. When poets use them, these metaphors can offer great resonance and depth to our images, without overtaking a line, stanza, or portion of a poem.

Implied metaphor   does not actually state in the comparison what our main object is being compared to; rather, it implies the comparison usually through action or ascribing attributes.

Extended or *controlling metaphor*   extends itself throughout an entire poem and becomes the controlling force behind the poem, the context by which we come to understand the poem.

The *extended* or *controlling metaphor* is another useful and powerful tool. It gets its name because this type of metaphor extends itself throughout an entire poem. And because of this, it becomes the controlling force behind the poem, the context by which we come to understand what the poet is trying to say. One superb example of this is Alice Walker's poem "A Woman Is Not a Potted Plant" wherein the metaphor of a woman being potted, trimmed, watered or not watered, clipped back, etcetera serves to illustrate her thoughts on how women have been treated in the world.

A Woman Is Not a Potted Plant
by Alice Walker

A WOMAN IS NOT
A POTTED PLANT

her roots bound
to the confines
of her house

a woman is not
a potted plant
her leaves trimmed
to the contours
of her sex

a woman is not
a potted plant
her branches
espaliered
against the fences
of her race
her country
her mother
her man

her trained blossom
turning
this way
& that
to follow
the sun
of whoever feeds
and waters
her

a woman
is wilderness
unbounded
holding the future
between each breath
walking the earth
only because
she is free
and not creepervine
or tree.

Nor even honeysuckle
or bee.

Another element of metaphor that poets employ is *personification,* which is giving a nonhuman object some human characteristic. For example, *the wind tiptoes through the trees.* Or in another case, *he swatted at air/the wasp*

Personification is giving a nonhuman or inanimate object some human characteristic.

laughed and dove again. The use of personification helps to bring alive for us those things outside our human world and makes these other realms understandable to us. As well, they help add to the zest of an image by allowing the author to be original and fresh in the construction of images.

Symbolism

Put simply, *symbolism* is an element of imagery employed by the poet in order to embed meaning into a poem beneath the literal surface of the words. A symbol is a concrete object that functions exactly as it *is* but also means something greater, wider at an abstract level. We have symbols all around us. Take a car for instance. If we associate wealth with cars, we might do a little free association. Ferrari—young, fast car wealth. Volvo—used to be a hippy, now a yuppie money. Rolls Royce—old money, so rich I have a driver money. You get the idea. In these examples, the car is still a car, but it tells us something about the person who owns it. In a poem, a symbol functions based on the context that is set up around the object. In the following poem by William Stafford, we have a car. The car may simply be a car, but we also might view the car as a symbol of technology, the industrial world and its collision with nature. And from there we might draw other conclusions about the poem. Also note the personification of the car, some of the language that Stafford uses to make it a being, and how that might affect our interpretation of it.

Symbolism   is an element of imagery whereby meaning is embedded into a poem beneath the literal usage of the words by using a symbol or symbols. A symbol is a concrete object which functions exactly as it *is* but also means or suggests something greater within the context of the poem, wider at an abstract level by reason of relationship or association.

Traveling through the Dark
by William Stafford

Traveling through the dark I found a deer
dead on the edge of the Wilson River road.
It is usually best to roll them into the canyon:
that road is narrow; to swerve might make more dead.

By glow of the tail-light I stumbled back of the car
and stood by the heap, a doe, a recent killing;
she had stiffened already, almost cold.
I dragged her off; she was large in the belly.

My fingers touching her brought me the reason—
her side was warm; her fawn lay there waiting,

alive, still, never to be born.
Beside that mountain road I hesitated.

The car aimed ahead its lowered parking lights;
under the hood purred the steady engine.
I stood in the glare of the warm exhaust turning red;
around our group I could hear the wilderness listen.

I thought hard for us all—my only swerving—,
then pushed her over the edge into the river.

Imagery is one of the elements most needed by poets and vital to the language that brings alive a poem for the reader. Like a river appearing calm on the surface while the current is moving sand and stones beneath, images can awaken our senses, stir us, move us deeply while staying relatively calm and placid in the poem. And often the best images, those which are concrete and detailed, say more implicitly than they do explicitly. As Ernest Gaines said in a workshop I attended once, "You know, I like writers who just show me things," because it's the writer's duty to show us the world and not tell us about it. And that's the way many poets proceed. Writers worry about showing the world and crafting the details carefully; when they do, they catch the wonder, bring on the shortness of breath, the skip of the heart to the reader. It's our heart and their duty to move it.

Point of View

One of the responsibilities of the poet, a writer of any sort, is to not beat up on people with language—we get that enough in the day to day world. So, writers need to be honest with how they come at things. Now, that doesn't mean poets can't alter their experiences or tell half-truths—as long as they represent real experiences then we're alright. What I'm talking about is tricking the readers, deceiving them, making them believe something they shouldn't. Raymond Carver used to say, "When I'm reading, at the first sign of a trick, I'm running for cover." So, it's up to the poet to capture experiences and relay the intellectual and emotional power behind them so that the readers feel they have experienced the world in a real and honest way. Writers do this for us by creating a speaker in a poem who can convey experience powerfully.

This speaker of a poem is called the *persona,* and he or she is the one who takes on the point of view in a poem. The *point of view* is the stance taken by the persona, the attitude, and the view of the world he imparts to the reader. Technically speaking, there are three types of point of view: first

Persona   is the speaker of the poem, the one who takes on the point of view in a poem.

Point of view   is the stance taken by the persona, the attitude, and the view of the world he imparts to the reader.

person (I/we), second person (you), and third person (he/she/it/they). These points of view also carry a ticket into the subject. Sometimes the persona (the narrator in fiction) will be *omniscient,* meaning all-knowing. Or the persona might be limited to knowing only certain details of the surroundings, characters, or things in the poem; this is *limited* point of view. Along with this stance and attitude comes the *tone*—the emotional sense behind the voice of the persona. As readers, we may not understand initially who the speaker is—persona or poet. Or we may not understand why the persona happens to be the one narrating the experience, which usually comes from some tension in the relationship between persona and place or experience. But this persona will create or fit into the context of the poem so it seems real. Let's take a situation. A Caucasian man and an American Indian woman walk into a restaurant in, say, any rural area near where you live. They are hungry and want to have breakfast. They wait at the chrome framed sign that says "Please Wait To Be Seated." No one comes to seat them. There are only two tables in the place being served. The rest are empty. Finally, the man says to the host, "Can we just go ahead and sit down?" The host glares a little and then comes up next to the white man and says—"We don't serve your type here." Thoughts swirl. What exactly does he mean? *Her* type or *our* type? The host is a racist. The Caucasian man thinks *let's beat the hell out of him.* The American Indian woman can't stand the behavior but decides it's best to just leave. What do we say? The couple leaves and as they do the waitress gives them a sympathetic and pleading look like "I'm so sorry, he's a horrible man."

Tone   of a poem is the emotional condition behind the voice of the persona.

Alright, there's our situation. Now, if we're the poet and we want to write a poem about it, first we have to decide who should tell the story. Should it be first person (I/me), second person (using "you" and addressing some other being seemingly reading the poem), or third person (he/she)? And of course it could be third person limited where our persona/speaker of the poem knows only limited details about what's happened or it could be omniscient where the persona knows all—maybe even knows that this man did the same thing only half an hour earlier. So, let's say the poet decides on first person. Now, she has one more consideration, and this is an important one. Who should be the persona—the man, the American Indian woman, or the waitress? Examining this question will show us how the connection between the persona/the experience/the context of place and time all help to build the evocative power of a poem. We have a different poem for each person in this situation. For years, the waitress has seen this man act this way. The white man is stunned and hasn't experienced either the man or the depth of racism and oppression either of the women have and especially the American Indian woman. But he's empathic and in a relationship with her. The American Indian woman on the other hand, has seen it before, can't stand it, wants to collar the restaurant host, but has enough control from having endured it, to walk right out the door. All of these points of view bring up very different emotional, intellectual, and psychological stances in the poem.

What comes of all this? We need to remember that our persona is the spokesperson for the psychological reality that plays out in the poem. And in this psychological reality, the kernel of the poem gets delivered, the truth of the poem gets handled. As readers, we must remember that the reality of a poem, or *truth* of a poem, is exactly that—the truth of that particular poem. Sometimes it may be directly about the poet's life, but at other times a poem may be slightly fictional or picked up from someone else's life. Hence, readers need to be careful to distinguish between the persona and the poet. Needless to say, in this example, there is a different truth to each possible persona. The poet needs to decide what truth it is she wants to tell, what truth it is she knows best, and what truth she can best show the reader. (And by best showing and telling the experiences, the reader can know that the person and point of view for the experience will offer fresh insights, some surprise for us.) For instance, we all probably expect the poem to be told from either the man or woman's point of view. The least expected point of view is the waitress'. But maybe that's the freshest poem. Provided the writer can evoke the depth of experience she wants from the waitress, then we have a fresh approach.

In the following poem by Robert Hayden, we have an example that is not quite as explosive as the above example. But note how the choice of persona and point of view help render the power of the poem and the kernel of truth and reality which become exposed. You might also note that there is no gender ascribed to the persona, and it seems as if this has an effect of opening the poem to us.

Those Winter Sundays
by Robert Hayden

Sundays too my father got up early
and put his clothes on in the blueblack cold,
then with cracked hands that ached
from labor in the weekday weather made
banked fires blaze. No one ever thanked him.

I'd wake and hear the cold splintering, breaking.
When the rooms were warm, he'd call,
and slowly I would rise and dress,
fearing the chronic angers of that house,

Speaking indifferently to him,
who had driven out the cold
and polished my good shoes as well.
What did I know, what did I know
of love's austere and lonely offices? (A/P)

When writers decide who will tell their poems, the voices of those characters in a poem, when they listen to the voices that come through to us (the readers), then they will craft a powerfully spoken poem. And we need to pay close attention to the speakers too. Poets will try to choose the voice that can express moments in ways that are natural and honest—the voice that recreates the world—so that what was once private to them becomes a shared and sensational moment to the reader. The poet might just pull us down the throats of speakers and into their hearts.

To Experience

1. Take an abstract word and write it on the top of a sheet of paper. Using only concrete details, write three to six lines using an image to illustrate that abstract concept, but do not use the abstract word or any others in the image. Use the following example as a guide.

   Sad
   The wind howls
   and rain presses against the backs of clouds.
   Leaves run and hide under bushes.
   All this while the bagpipe screams.

2. To explore metaphor (extended/controlling metaphor), look at Alice Walker's poem in this chapter. Take any of the kinds of plants she uses—potted, trimmed, espaliered, etcetera. What type of woman is she portraying? That is to say, what type of woman is society trying to grow or make? Which words function to drive the extended metaphor?

To Write

1. After reading William Stafford's poem "Traveling through the Dark," write a short essay or journal entry discussing how symbolism helps make sense of our "real" world. You might consider how a tension arises between the objects functioning as symbols and the reality of the narrative in the poem.

2. Discuss in an essay or journal entry how you think the persona feels about his situation in Robert Hayden's poem "Those Winter Sundays." You might specifically discuss what words in the poem lead you to your conclusions about the persona's mood and tone.

Chapter Five

Sound and the Poem:

Can You Hear It?

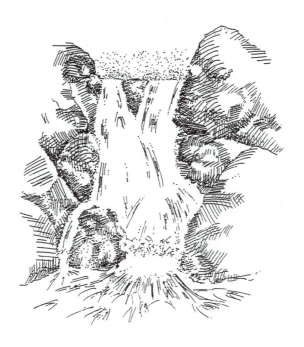

Sound is everywhere. It is around us constantly, and we are regularly moved or startled or taken by sound. Take, for example, the crashing together of two train cars coupling at the rail yard, the crunching of a can under a girl's foot, the fast panting of a dog in the shade of a tree, the screech of tires against asphalt, the plunk of a rock in a pond. These sounds we know; maybe we hear them every day depending on who we are and where we live. Often we don't think of them as poetic. But, we have reactions to these sounds when we do hear them. Sound is something that moves us—it can frighten us, relax us, and delight us. And because of this, the poet will attempt to capture the sounds around us in words, adding them to the sensory experience a reader encounters in a poem.

As you rub these words together they spark and whole new combinations happen.

Naomi Shihab Nye

In our daily lives, we have learned to hear sounds and move right past them or through them. In fact, we've learned to hear without performing an attentive act of listening. And yet the same magic that is held in imagery is held in sound. But, we need to slow down and listen momentarily to catch it. Of course, this is what's happening in a poem—the writer temporarily slows the reader in a moment in order to show us what is important. The sound might be presented simply in one line as something no more than the lids of pots clanging together like a bell. We should note that in their attempt to capture the world, the poet has presented the sound, taken the time to create a whole sensory experience for us. The reader should feel a freshness in hearing the world—in some cases for the first time—because often we are entering the poet's world through the poem for the first time. We should be captivated. We should turn to say, "how beautiful" or "how ear scraping" or "I've never thought of it that way before."

The Creation of Sound in a Poem

Poets will create sound in two ways: 1) Through careful word choice they will capture and create the sounds of the world; and 2) they will create sonic effects in the poem . . . through the inherent sounds in words created by consonants, vowels, and stressed or unstressed syllables. So, when choosing words for poems the poet will consider how they will function in the poem and what meanings will emerge from them. Through diction and other conventions such as rhyme, rhythm, and meter, the poet creates connections between words that develop meaning and enhance our reading experience in the poem.

These conventions are largely technical, and they are the tools for creating sound. We need them and we need to know how they work and what they do for us. But, when a poet writes, they tend to show up a bit more naturally, or organically, than we might think. So, if they show up naturally, why do we need to know them as tools? We need to know them as tools because when a poet revises the sound doesn't just blossom onto the page—the poet works to place sound quality into the poem. Though for a reader this should all be transparent. We should hear things in the poem, but we should also know if we go back to analyze the poem that the poet has most certainly strained to embed it with sound to enhance the poem's effect.

Let's start by talking a bit about consonant and vowel sounds in words. Alliteration, consonance, and assonance are poetic elements that arise from the use of consonants and vowels. *Alliteration* is the repetition of consonant

Alliteration   is the repetition of consonant sounds which usually occurs at the beginning of words and produces an echo effect thereby linking words through their sounds.

sounds and usually occurs at the beginning of words, which produces an echo effect as well as linking words through their sounds. For example, *the friends fought.* Or in another case, *the snake silently slithered away.* Alliteration is a common tool—next time you sit down to write think about it and make a point to use it, and you will also begin to see it in the poems you read. Poets also employ *consonance,* which is the repetition of consonant sounds in closely placed words. For example, we might have the words *slumber* and *member* and what we hear in this is that the consonant sounds in the middle and end of each word are the same. *Assonance* is the repetition of vowel sounds in words and also produces an effect similar to alliteration or consonance. It is a partial rhyme. The vowel sounds are the same but the consonant sounds differ. For example, with *blunder* and *slumber,* in both cases, the repetition of sounds causes the words to blend together closely through sound and meaning. What's more, assonance and consonance are the root forces at work when we discuss rhyme and are used by poets to create an effect that stimulates our aural sense.

Consonance   is the repetition of consonant sounds in closely placed words.

Assonance   is the repetition of vowel sounds in words and also produces an effect similar to alliteration or consonance. It is a partial rhyme. The vowel sounds are the same but the consonant sounds may differ.

Rhyme

Now that we know what makes rhyme happen, let's look at some types of rhyme we have. *Rhyme* is an echoing produced by close placement of two or more words with similarly sounding final syllables. There are a number of types of rhyme all producing various *rhythms.* There is *masculine rhyme* in which two words end with the same vowel consonant combination (hand/band); *feminine rhyme* in which two syllables rhyme (shiver/liver); *end rhyme* in which the rhyme comes at the end of the lines (this is a traditional and commonly used rhyme); and *internal rhyme* in which a word within a line rhymes with another word in that line or at the end or rhymes with a word of similar placement in the following line.

Rhythm   is the music formed by stressed and unstressed syllables in a line.

Masculine rhyme   is when two words end with the same vowel consonant combination.

Feminine rhyme   is when two syllables rhyme.

End rhyme   is when the rhyme comes at the end of the lines.

Internal rhyme   is when a word within a line rhymes with another word in that line or at the end or rhymes with a word of similar placement in the following line.

There is also a type of rhyme called *slant rhyme* in which the sounds nearly rhyme but are not a "true rhyme" (land/lend). And finally there is what we call *sight rhyme* where the words look alike but do not sound alike (hood/blood).

Slant rhyme   is when the sounds nearly rhyme but are not a "true rhyme."

Sight rhyme   is where the words look alike but do not sound alike.

Now that we know what types of rhyme we see and hear, let's talk briefly about what rhyme does and why it's used at all. Rhyme can do a few things for a poet and her poems. First, rhyme can help a poet measure lengths of verse, either line by line or in larger chunks of language. It can do this by setting up recurrent points of rest in the language. Second, because the poet might measure off language, rhyme can help set a rhythm to the language we are using. And, third, rhyme can help words become glued together in their sound and meaning so the poem gains a quality that is both pleasing to the ear and intellectually or emotionally stimulating. At its best, rhyme, does not beat us over the head—in fact we may read right past it or it may help us to read, guiding us musically through the poem, taking us up and setting us down in all the appropriate places. Let's look at how much rhyme is employed in the following poem by Maxine Kumin but without the rhyme overtaking the sound of the poem.

Woodchucks

by Maxine Kumin

Gassing the woodchucks didn't turn out right.
The knockout bomb from the Feed and Grain Exchange
was featured as merciful, quick at the bone
and the case we had against them was airtight,
both exits shoehorned shut with puddingstone,
but they had a sub-sub-basement out of range.

Next morning they turned up again, no worse
for the cyanide than we for our cigarettes
and state-store Scotch, all of us up to scratch.
They brought down the marigolds as a matter of course
and then took over the vegetable patch
nipping the broccoli shoots, beheading the carrots.

The food from our mouths, I said, righteously thrilling
to the feel of the .22, the bullets' neat noses.
I, a lapsed pacifist fallen from grace
puffed with Darwinian pieties for killing,

now drew a bead on the littlest woodchuck's face.
He died down in the everbearing roses.

Ten minutes later I dropped the mother. She
flipflopped in the air and fell, her needle teeth
still hooked in a leaf of early Swiss chard.
Another baby next. O one-two-three
the murderer inside me rose up hard,
the hawkeye killer came on stage forthwith.

There's one chuck left. Old wily fellow, he keeps
me cocked and ready day after day after day.
All night I hunt his humped-up form. I dream
I sight along the barrel in my sleep.
If only they'd all consented to die unseen
gassed underground the quiet Nazi way.

As we read "Woodchucks," these sounds drive the poem in a very transparent way. For instance, you may not have even noticed that in Ms.
Kumin's poem she employs rhyme at the end of lines. And the internal
rhyme is plentiful throughout each stanza. All of this helps to pace the
poem, create a gentle momentum, and glue words together by heighten-
ing the way we hear them in the poetic context of their meaning. What
this creates is a sense of following this true to life, if humorous, poem until we're slapped at the end with the serious historical underpinning. We
might ask after our first read, "How did I miss that?" But upon another
few readings, we see that the focus on imagery, rhyme, rhythm, and pacing in the poem keeps us focused on the moment of the farm and the tension within our persona.

Finally, another element of sound to consider is *onomatopoeia,* when a
word sounds like or resembles what it is. For instance, *a snake <u>hisses</u>* or for
another example, *the wood fell with a <u>thud</u> into the ground.* We can come up
with a number of examples like *buzz, rattle, honk,* and more. This is a very
effective tool for sound because the poet may use onomatopoeia to act on its
own or may find very original ways to couple words and enhance a rhyming
effect. Along with these aforementioned tools, it can be important to consider
the number of syllables in words that come together in lines and stanzas, next
to each other or on top of each other in different lines. Considering syllables
alongside alliteration, assonance, and onomatopoeia can combine to produce
euphony or cacophony in poems. *Euphony* is the blending of sounds into a

Onomatopoeia   is when a word sounds like or resembles what it is. For example the
    word hiss actually has a hiss embedded in its sound.

pleasurable effect on the ear while *cacophony* has the opposite effect and produces a noisy or unpleasant effect on us. This may happen from the true
sound of the word, the word's meaning, or it may happen based on line structure and a group of words. For example, in James Wright's lines "the cowbells follow one another/into the distances of the afternoon," these cowbells
are not breaking apart our afternoon with their clanging. In fact, by them following one another into the distance they are actually getting quieter. They
are producing some sense of relaxation.

Euphony   is the blending of sounds into a pleasurable effect on the ear. This may happen
from the true sound of the word, the word's meaning, or it may happen based on the
rhythm of line structure and/or word groupings.

Cacophony   is when a word (or words) produces a noisy or unpleasant effect. This may
happen from the true sound of the word, the word's meaning, or it may happen
based on the rhythm of line structure and/or word groupings.

While these technical conventions of sound need to be thought about
consciously, we should also allow them to just be in the poem and work on
us without looking for them. Just read and know they are there. And, we
can remember that a poet uses these tools when crafting a poem, and they
will usually follow this maxim—never force or impose a convention on the
poem. So, when we work back to analyze a poem, to explicate how and why
it might work and what it means, we need to remember that these forces are
at work in a natural, fluid manner. Remember that these effects help enhance images and the whole of a poem. In the following poem by Richmond
Lattimore, notice how the sonic words create power in the poem by building the images of the poem and the tension felt by us through the persona.
The sounds of the poem work against the anticipated sympathy we'll have
for the crabs.

The Crabs
by Richmond Lattimore

There was a bucket full of them. They spilled,
crawled climbed, clawed: slowly tossed
and fell: precision made: cold iodine color of their own
world of sand and occasional brown weed, round stone
chilled clean in the chopping waters of their coast.
One fell out. The marine thing on the grass
tried to trundle off, barbarian and immaculate and to be killed
with his kin. We lit water: dumped the living mass
in: contemplated tomatoes and corn: and with the good cheer of
civilized man,
cigarettes, that is, and cold beer and chatter,

waited out and lived down the ten-foot-away clatter
of crabs as they died for us inside their boiling can.

Lines & Stanzas

In understanding differences between poetry and prose, one of the things
most identifiable to readers is the difference between how the two look on
the page. Other than the prose poem, we can look at a poem and identify it
as such. While this is a very basic tool to identify a poem, it works. But, what
we are identifying as different is not just an insignificant part of a poem;
rather, *lines* and *stanzas* are major elements in poetics. So, as a reader, it's
important to understand what they might do for a poem. A line is just that—
it's a line of text in a poem. A stanza is a group of two or more lines set together in a poem and often arranged around a metrical or rhythmic pattern.
And in poetry we will find that a poem may be all one stanza or it may be
divided into, say, six four-line stanzas.

Line   is a line of text in a poem.

Stanza   is a group of two or more lines set together in a poem and often arranged around
a metrical, conceptual, or rhythmic pattern.

Now that we know what they are, let's talk a bit about how and why
a poet uses lines and stanzas to affect their poems. Lines and stanzas occur
often in a very natural, organic way. In other words, the lines or stanzas
form naturally and the poet is paying attention to breaks in lines or groupings of lines driven by the content and the inherent rhythms of the language. So, lines happen because the writer decided to break phrases the
way she thinks or feels the words. And stanzas may occur because she feels
a group of lines works well together conceptually. But, let's take a closer
look at lines.

Lines

Lines do a number of things in a poem both spatially and conceptually. In
relation to space on the page, the way words appear, lines provide a spatial
context in which the words function. This is initially the way the words look
on the page, the way we see them. But as we read the poem, it becomes not
just how they look on the page but how the words work with and against
each other in the reading process. For example, note the difference in the two
examples of the following lines.

The wind swept
off the dunes and raced
against the waves,
pulling their white hair
out away from shore.

Here, we have five lines broken ostensibly to show the images in each line. But note that the lines begin with an article, prepositions, and a gerund. These are not bad choices, but consider the possibilities. Think how many ways the writer might break them. Let's look at a revision of these lines.

> The wind swept off the dunes and
> raced against the waves, pulling
> their white hair out away from shore.

The first thing we might notice is that we get longer lines in this choice of line breaks. We might also notice a change in the rhythm of the language. Having the words "and" and "pulling" at the end of the lines doesn't seem natural. But, it may also create a sense of tension in the language or a sense that the wind is working against the natural rhythm of the waves. We might also note that this line structure seems to complement the internal rhyme in lines two and three a bit more than the previous line scheme. No matter the changes, notice that the line acts as a frame of emphasis and causes us to subtly, even subconsciously, focus on different emotions, thoughts, and/or parts of the poem with each change. The line is a place for the words to take on a collective connection. This means that as a reader we must be constantly vigilant through every moment of the poem.

This brings us to another point about lines and their function. Lines provide the poet a way to create or control the rhythm and musical sense of the poem. They provide for us the length of breath we might need, or the number of syllables working together in a unit of words, or lines may set up a recurrent rhythmic pattern. When we look at a poem, we know enough to say something like, "It has short lines so it must be a poem." Or maybe we read a bit and we say "It's a poem because it rhymes." We are intuitively noting what we believe makes a poem. And we're right on both counts. One of the central forces behind the language in a poem is its rhythm. We learn this young. We hear things like:

> The wood mouse, the wood mouse
> ran into the house.
> But when he found the crock of lard
> he knew that he would starve.

Or something like these lines:

> Hinx, minx, the old witch stinks
> the fat begins to fry.
> Nobody's home, nobody's home
> but mother and father and I.

And so we realize that the short lines, rhyme, and rhythm help make a poem. First, *rhythm* is the music formed by stressed and unstressed sylla-

---

Rhyme   is an echoing produced by close placement of two or more words with similarly sounding final syllables.

bles in a line. This is very subtle in poems but is the undercurrent to what we hear and feel in a musical sense.

There are two main ways rhythm comes to be in a poem: syllabic rhythm or meter. First let's have a look at syllables generating rhythm. One way to play with this, as you think about line breaks, is to simply count syllables in lines. If you have three lines of roughly six syllables each, how is that different than two lines of nine syllables each? And then we might look at where the stressed syllables fall and where the unstressed syllables fall. And we know that stressed and unstressed syllables in words don't change—those are a constant. So, when a poet changes the rhythm of a line by making it longer or breaking it to be shorter, she not only alters the meaning of the words by shifting the frame within which they function, but she shifts the music of the poem.

One element of line breaks that affects rhythm is the caesura. A *caesura* is simply a pause within a line, usually occurring because of punctuation, that breaks the regularity of the rhythmic or metrical pattern. But a caesura may also happen because of the way two words fall next to each other rhythmically. In this case, don't be fooled into thinking it's a difficult technique. The caesura works something like a rest between notes in music. Just keep in mind that this is what pauses within a line are called and rhythmically they can make all the difference at times. A second element of line structure relative to syntax, rhythm, and meaning is *enjambment*. This is when a sentence, or sense of a phrase, does not stop at the end of a line in either its grammatical sense or its meaning. Hence, the sentence runs through the end of one line and into the next. This is not overly technical, but enjambment allows a poet the room to create a rhythmic pattern while having room to carry the meaning of the language from one line to another. As you become more and more aware of how it and other elements are subtle forces in the lines of a poem, you are creating a deft ability to analyze meaning and apply interpretations.

Caesura   is a pause within a line, usually occurring because of punctuation, that breaks the regularity of the rhythmic or metrical pattern.

Enjambment   is when a sentence, or sense of a phrase, does not stop at the end of a line in either its grammatical sense or its meaning.

Meter

Another way to achieve the musical movement of a line or lines, is through meter. First, *meter* is the arrangement of measured rhythm in poetry (*measured* is a key word here and you might think of how music is

Meter   is the arrangement of measured rhythm in poetry and this measurement happens based on where the stressed and unstressed syllables are in words.

measured). This measurement happens based on where the stressed and unstressed syllables are in words. On one hand, that makes it easy because the stressed syllables and the unstressed syllables in words don't change—they are what they are. But meter becomes a bit more complicated as we put a number of words together. As well, meter is measured in what are called feet. And a *foot* is one measurement of stressed and unstressed syllables. Now, types of meter are based on these measurements.

Types of Feet in Poetic Meter

iamb	ă é
trochee	é ă
anapest	ă ă é
dactyl	é ă ă
spondee	é é

The above examples are the types of feet there are in poetry. When we place these in lines and begin to have a number of feet working together, then we find a type of recurring meter (you may know the term iambic pentameter, for instance). Within these types of feet we have what we refer to as rising and falling meter. *Rising meter* is when we go from unstressed syllables to stressed syllables. Therefore the iamb and the anapest are rising meters. *Falling meter* is just the opposite—we go from stressed to unstressed. The trochee and the dactyl are feet with falling meter.

Foot   is a measurement of stressed and unstressed syllables.

Rising meter   is when a foot moves from unstressed syllables to stressed syllables.

Falling meter   is when a foot moves from stressed to unstressed syllables.

In a single line of poetry when there is one foot, it is called *monometer;* when there are two feet, it is called *dimeter;* when there are three feet, it is called *trimeter;* four feet is called *tetrameter;* five feet is called *pentameter;* six feet is called *hexameter;* seven feet is called *heptameter;* and eight feet is called *octameter.* And so to get the name of a meter, we couple the type of foot with the number of feet in a line (hence iambic pentameter for a line with five iambs). To illustrate meter at work,

Monometer   is when a single line of poetry has one foot.

Dimeter   is when a single line of poetry has two feet.

Trimeter   is when a single line of poetry has three feet.

Tetrameter   is when a single line of poetry has four feet.

Pentameter   is when a single line of poetry has five feet.

Hexameter   is when a single line of poetry has six feet.

Heptameter   is when a single line of poetry has seven feet.

Octameter   is when a single line of poetry has eight feet.

let's look at the poem "My Papa's Waltz" by Theodore Roethke's. This is a relatively common meter, but rather than telling you what it is, see if you can figure it out on your own.

My Papa's Waltz

by Theodore Roethke

The whiskey on your breath
Could make a small boy dizzy;
But I hung on like death:
Such waltzing was not easy.

We romped until the pans
Slid from the kitchen shelf;
My mother's countenance
Could not unfrown itself.

The hand that held my wrist
Was battered on one knuckle;
At every step you missed
My right ear scraped a buckle.

You beat time on my head
With a palm caked hard by dirt,
Then waltzed me off to bed
Still clinging to your shirt.

Something to note with this poem is that Mr. Roethke must have chosen this meter because it closely mimics the beat of the waltz. Hence, the meter seems very natural in the poem and rises out of the content of the poem—it is not imposed. So, we might argue that Mr. Roehtke couldn't have written this poem any other way.

Now to illustrate a falling meter, here is a line of trochaic tetrameter, meaning the line has a stressed/ unstressed foot (the trochee) and it recurs four times (the tetrameter).

Fighting / was her / huge ob / session;
she threw / pitchers / at her / husband.

Notice that the last foot of the first line breaks in the middle of a word. This a reasonable thing to do when constructing meter and provides poets some latitude in word choice and line structure.

This may seem technical, and to use a car metaphor, this is like understanding the strokes of cylinders. In poetry where we want a strict meter, and especially in poetic forms where poets pay close attention to recurring metrical patterns, the beats in each foot of each line are like the spark plugs firing inside the engine. With a well tuned line the poem runs smoothly. But, then again, let's remember that a poet might actually break the recurring meter for effect.

In the end, meter provides a sense of rhythm which is recurrent. At the least (say in nursery rhymes), meter provides us a sense of beat and music and bodily pleasure. If we use it to mirror what is happening in images it might be used to create the natural rhythms that are taking place—say, a horse galloping or people dancing. Remember Theodore Roethke's poem "My Papa's Waltz" wherein the meter of the line mimics the waltz and even mimics when the father misses a step. At its best, skillfully used meter gets woven into the subtleties of the language. It gets used according to the natural cadences of speech, the meanings of words, and the way in which language is portrayed in a poem.

The Stanza

A *stanza* is a group of two or more lines set together in a poem and often arranged around a metrical or rhythmic pattern. In free verse, these groups of lines do not need to be the same in number, but when a stanza occurs it is usually always doing the same job—it signifies that there is some type of organizational structure to the words, lines, and poem. Often a writer organizes lines into stanzas based on some conceptual coherence. No matter how many stanzas a poem has or how those stanzas occur in the poem (maybe some have three lines, maybe some have four, maybe all have two), the stanza serves to provide some sense of coherence to the lines. The movements between stanzas help guide us smoothly through the meaning of the poem. I sometimes hear inexperienced poetry students make the comment, "in the fourth paragraph of the poem. . . " Well, I'll correct them so they're using the right terminology. But, the mistake is understandable—they see the stanza as acting like a paragraph. And in fact it does in some ways. It often houses lines of similar content, and it typically has a sense of unity and coherence. However, that unity and coherence are often driven not simply by meaning but by a number of poetic elements, including rhythm, working together in the stanza.

In fixed form poems, stanzaic structure is guided by the type of poem (sonnet, sestina, villanelle, etc.), the dominant meter (for instance, iambic pentameter or tetrameter), and the rhyme scheme. For example, a four-line stanza with iambic pentameter, and a rhyme scheme of *abab* might be used as the first stanza of a sonnet. The use of stanzas and their fixed structures in formed poems helps give a framework to the poem as well as a technical context wherein the content functions. But, let's go back to free verse.

So, in free verse, why use stanzas at all? Sometimes a poet uses only one stanza. But that too has a history and comes from the *stichic* tradition of poetry or arranging a poem by lines rather than the stanza being a guiding force. This simply means that the lines fall into one unit and are arranged more by their rhythmic quality than being separated into stanzas based on either number or meaning. So, why break parts of the poem with white space? One reason a poet uses stanzas is that she can control what she wants to say. In some ways, it's not all that different than a conversation. And, after all, in many ways poets are having a conversation with readers. In conversation, when we change subject or even alter it by nuance—maybe where we're going is still deeply related but we're taking a turn—we note this in some way. A pause, a change in tone, a change in breath. These are all things that can be set off by stanza breaks. Hence, as a reader, we must use stanzas as a guide. Looking at it with a bit more severity, we might say that the poet sometimes controls the poem through stanzas. So, the reader might use the stanza as a means to control some sense of analysis of the poem.

What comes of this control, this movement of lines and subject matter, of rhythms and breath, is a control over the dynamics of the poem. With stanzas the poet takes on the ability to bring the poem up to crescendo-like levels and then ease it back down again. To run the poem full speed like a train or slow it down. When a poet takes the poem up to a high point and brings it down again with the use of stanzas, she ought to do this because the subject matter calls for it. This way the stanzas fit, they're in the right place at the right time, but they seem transparent to the readers—we hardly notice. But we notice how the poem feels, what the poem means. The stanzas, their structure and movement, ought to mirror or enhance the subject matter or the emotional/intellectual stance of the poem.

One of the things poets do with lines and stanzas, as Robert Hass points out, is that a poet puts their breathing, their own physical, rhythmic nature into other people's bodies. "When one says somebody else's poem aloud, one speaks in that person's breath." This is where body, line, and stanza meet and help create the poetic voice on the page. Listen to the movement of the language; hear the rhythms around you, the dance on the page, these twirling steps of lines.

To Experience

1. Write something in prose without using any line breaks. Then go back and break the prose into lines. Once the writing is broken into lines, break it into stanzas. Pay close attention to where, when, and why you're breaking the language where you are.

2. Copy a poem of your choice, but write it out as a paragraph taking out all line and stanza breaks. Then without looking at the original go back through the poem and break it into lines. Then compare your version with the poet's version. Try to assess why you broke yours in certain places and why the poet broke theirs in certain places.

To Write

1. Choose a poem and write a short essay or journal entry focusing on lines and stanzas. Analyze how the lines and stanzas affect the rhythm or meter of the poem and how the lines, stanzas, and rhythm are connected to the meaning of the poem.

Chapter Six

Fixed Forms:

Shaping the Currents of Poetry

Traditionally, poetry was crafted through the use of forms. And it is only in our more recent past when poets have largely abandoned fixed forms such as the sonnet or sestina for the use of free verse or open form. As we've become more and more acquainted with free verse, many of us have a preference for it over formed poems. Possibly it's because a form seems rigid; maybe it's because form seems to us to have old trappings and we perceive it as "nothing new"; or we sense that we're going to be dragged through something we only half understand in its rules and all we want is the point of the poem. I'm as guilty of having felt this way as the next person. But usually it's because of some preconceived notion we have about form. If we remember that over the thousands of years poets have used fixed forms these forms have evolved and have been creatively altered, then

"Don't let anyone persuade you. . .
that form is not substance to that
degree that there is absolutely no
substance without it."

Henry James

we will remember that even poets working in forms are on the creative edge, working toward something new and exciting. And if we come to know just a bit about the form we're reading, we have a greater likelihood of seeing it from the poet's eye, from a stance of possibility and wonder. We can watch the meaning of the poem unfold from within the form.

A *fixed form* poem is one that conforms to a set pattern of lines, stanzas, rhyme, and/or meter. These patterns vary from form to form and may or may not require patterns in all of these categories. For instance, the villanelle doesn't require a set pattern of line length but the sonnet does. Though historically, poets throughout the world have largely conformed to patterns in their poems, to fixed forms, they have not done it without attempting change, alterations, and movements in the forms based on the creative practice of their time. Our modern and contemporary writers may have seemed to abandon form altogether, but we should remember that most poets have been schooled in forms—they just don't always work in them. And when they do, they may look for ways that the form can be slightly altered in order to fit style, diction, or subject choice. One of America's great mid-twentieth century poets and teachers of poetry, Theodore Roethke noted for us that "Our deepest perceptions are a waste if we have no sense of form." Mr. Roethke is putting great trust in the intelligence of the poet—and why not. He is certain that the poet will have something to say. But Mr. Roethke is delivering a great caveat that the poet ought to know how to say it in order to say it well. This meeting of form and content is what we refer to as *organic form*. In other words, a writer will not simply decide to write a sonnet; rather, they will choose the right form for the subject matter. Therefore, a poet never imposes a form on their subject. The subject and meaning of the poem come forth from inside the form naturally. In its most extreme, this scenario means that there is really only one way to write the poem—if the poem is screaming out to be a villanelle, it could never be a good sonnet.

Fixed form   poem is one that conforms to a set pattern of lines, stanzas, rhyme, and/or meter designated by a fixed structure for a poem.

In examining forms, we'll pay close attention to line length and meter as the rhythm of the line set up the number of feet in each line. And we'll look closely at rhyme scheme. When we have multiple rhymes in a poem, we signify patterns by using letters: the first rhyme is *a*; the second rhyme is *b*; the third rhyme is *c*; and so forth. Hence, poems might have various patterns, which look something like *aabb ccdd* or *abba cddc*. And the grouping of these letters together signifies the stanzas. In the stanza structure of fixed form poems, we will find that stanzas are referred to by the number of lines each has. A two-line stanza is called a *couplet;* a three-line stanza is a *tercet;* a four-line stanza is referred to as a *quatrain;* and a six-line stanza is referred to as a *sestet.* In this chapter, we'll look at four common fixed forms still widely practiced today and each having existed through the better part of our western literature and world canon: the sonnet, the villanelle, the haiku, and the elegy.

Couplet   is a two line stanza.

Tercet   is a three line stanza.

Quatrain   is a four line stanza.

Sestet   is a six line stanza.

The Sonnet

The sonnet is one of our more popular fixed forms having retained its appeal and vogue for over six centuries. It is an Italian form dating back to the thirteenth century and was used widely among the Italian court poets. Later, in the fourteenth century it reached a height of popularity through the poems of Petrarch. The Petrarchan sonnet heavily influenced early British poets, also court poets, who found the form a passionate and appropriate way to handle their subject du'jour, the various types and ranges of love. The *sonnet* is a 14 line poem usually set in five foot iambic lines. Rhyme schemes vary between the Italian tradition and the English tradition, largely because of the linguistic possibilities of rhyme, but also because of the difference in structure. The Petrarchan sonnet is set up in two parts, an octave (the first eight lines) and then a sestet (the last six lines). In the first eight lines, the poet sets up a problem, a question, or an emotional tension which is spoken to or answered in the last six lines or sestet. The octave is rhymed *abbaabba* while the sestet rhymes in various possibilities of *cdccdc, cdecde,* or *cdedce.* The English sonnet by contrast is usually structured into three quatrains and a couplet. While the meter of the lines remained a five foot iambic line, the rhyme scheme was often *abab cdcd efef gg.*

In the following sonnet by Sir Thomas Wyatt, we can note the Italian influence in his work as he follows the Petrarchan form closely. Wyatt was one of the early English sonneteers—alongside Henry Howard, Earl of Surrey

Sonnet   is a 14 line poem usually set in five foot iambic lines. Rhyme schemes vary between the Italian tradition and the English tradition, largely because of the linguistic possibilities of rhyme, but also because of the slight difference in structure.

and Sir Philip Sidney—and was influential in not only making the form popular in Britain as a court poet but in creatively setting up the groundwork for those later poets such as William Shakespeare and Edmund Spenser who solidified the English sonnet. In the following poem, note the use of the Petrarchan form and the rough use of the iambic line, a difference in Wyatt's style from his contemporary Surrey who often used a more tightly constructed five foot iambic line.

from Ten Sonnets

by Sir Thomas Wyatt

iii

Farewell, Love, and all thy laws forever:
Thy baited hooks shall tangle me no more.
Senec and Plato call me from thy lore,
To perfect wealth my wit for to endeavour.
In blind error when I did persever,
Thy sharp repulse, that pricketh aye so sore,
Hath taught me to set in trifles no store,
And scape forth, since liberty is lever.
Therefore, farewell, go trouble younger hearts,
and in me claim no more authority:
With idle youth go use thy property,
And thereon spend thy many brittle darts.
For hitherto tho' I've lost all my time,
Me lusteth no longer rotten boughs to climb.

In a more recent example of the sonnet, the following poem by contemporary American writer Donald Hall exhibits his use of the Petrarchan form. We can note with Hall's use of diction and the line that while he end rhymes, his use of enjambment forces us to read through the end of the line without a pause, thereby slightly de-emphasizing the rhyme. As well, while Hall employs the traditional subject of love in this sonnet it is not without a melancholic twist.

The Funeral

by Donald Hall

It is the box from which no jack will spring.
Now close the box, but not until she kisses
The crossed, large hands which she already misses
For their caress, and on his hand the ring.
Now close the box, if we close anything.

She sees the wooden lid, and she dismisses
At least a hundred thoughtful artifices
That would enjoy the tears that the would bring.

The coffin does not matter. It was one
Like many in the row from which she chose it.
Now to be closed in it, he must become
Like all other dead men, deaf and dumb,
Blank to the small particulars that stun
Her mind all day. Black men, now come and close it.

The Villanelle

The villanelle dates back to the fifteenth century but reached popularity in Europe in the sixteenth century. The word itself, villanelle, is derived from the Italian word *villanella* meaning a rustic song. Though accounts vary in their accuracy, some have it said that traveling bards and troubadours who helped popularize the form would use it as a means of gaining lodging for a night at villas by singing for the folks already there. Whether we want to believe these accounts or not, we can see how musical the structure is. The form is a strict and rigorous one which through its rhyme and line repetition produces a very songlike quality. The *villanelle* consists of nineteen lines divided into six stanzas. There are five tercets (three-line stanzas) and a final quatrain (four-line stanza). The rhyme scheme of the stanzas is *aba* for each of the tercets and *abaa* for the concluding quatrain. Further, the lines repeat in the following order: line one appears in the poem as lines six, twelve, and eighteen; and line three appears in the poem as lines nine, fifteen, and nineteen. It's this repetition that can cause the villanelle to take on almost chant-like qualities. And though the form does not require a line length of recurring metrical pattern, most poets attempt to build some sense of rhythm throughout the line with approximate syllable structure.

In the following poem by another mid-century American poet, Elizabeth Bishop, we can see that she has molded the form slightly. Bishop follows the form by repeating in its entirety (with only slight nuance) the first line of the poem. But when it comes to line three she uses only the word "disaster" as the echoing effect throughout the poem. And though it is seemingly only a small part of line three, its effect shows us how important that one word

Villanelle consists of nineteen lines divided into six stanzas. There are five tercets (three line stanzas) and a final quatrain (four line stanza). The rhyme scheme of the stanzas is *aba* for each of the tercets and *abaa* for the concluding quatrain. Further, the lines repeat in the following order: line 1 appears in the poem as lines 6, 12, and 18; and line 3 appears in the poem as lines 9, 15, and 19.

becomes for the entire poem. Moreover, she opens interpretive possibilities in the poem by relying on only one word instead of the entire line.

One Art
by Elizabeth Bishop

The art of losing isn't hard to master;
so many things seem filled with the intent
to be lost that their loss is no disaster.

Lose something every day. Accept the fluster
of lost door keys, the hour badly spent.
The art of losing isn't hard to master.

Then practice losing farther, losing faster:
places, and names, and where it was you meant
to travel. None of these will bring disaster.

I lost my mother's watch. And look! my last, or
next-to-last, of three loved houses went.
The art of losing isn't hard to master.

I lost two cities, lovely ones. And, vaster,
some realms I owned, two rivers, a continent.
I miss them, but it wasn't a disaster.

—Even losing you (the joking voice, a gesture
I love) I shan't have lied. It's evident
the art of losing's not too hard to master
though it may look like (*Write* it!) like disaster.

Haiku

The haiku is a poetic form out of the Japanese literary tradition that has transformed over hundreds of years to what it is today. The form rose out of other Japanese traditions, the *haikai* and the *hokku*. And, though a short poem, it contains strict rules which the poet must follow. Because of its length, haiku were often written in a series of one hundred poems. These series might be created by a single author but often haiku were constructed at parties where the participants would construct them together including not only attention to the surroundings but humor, as the *haikai* is a humorous form of poetry.

The *haiku* is a three line poem consisting of seventeen syllables following a line structure of five, seven, and five syllables and without requirements

Haiku   is a three line poem consisting of seventeen syllables following a line structure of five, seven, and five syllables and without requirements of rhyme.

of rhyme. Though only having three lines, there is a line function in the haiku. The first two lines typically capture some observation of the season, time of day, or an object(s) which form a representative image of a place. Then in the third line we may finish with another image or object coupled with an observation, sensation, or emotion. What typically happens is that between the second and third lines the poet makes a metaphorical leap like fording a river. And the only way to continue in the poem as a reader is to follow to the other side, which requires attention to the details in all three lines and a focused attention at forming connections between the lines. The tight lines and compression of language in the haiku allow the form to be exceptionally expressive; for the art of the haiku lies in expressing much in few words but suggesting even more.

from Narrow Road to the Interior
by Matsuo Basho trans. by Sam Hamill

Spring passes
and the birds cry out—
tears in the eyes of fishes

Ungraciously, under
a soldier's empty helmet
a cricket sings

The Elegy

The elegy in its classical dress was a form that adhered to very strict standards of rhyme and meter and stanza structure. Elegiac meter was a very complicated meter combining dactylic hexameter with a type of pentameter. And while it might be a poem or song expressing sorrow at some death, it was not always restricted to that subject. Classic poets wrote about love in the elegy to, but the elegy was really considered any poem written in elegiac meter. Now, though, the *elegy* has come to be regarded as a lyric poem written to commemorate someone's dying. Because a *lyric poem* is a poem that is designed to express the thoughts, reflections, or feelings of the poet or persona in the poem, the elegy expresses the sadness or epiphany connected with the death represented in the poem. In the following poem by Albert Garcia, we can see that he deals with a subject that we may all know but by adding an elegiac quality to the poem, he creates a fresh approach to the subject and places us in the tension the persona experiences.

Elegy   has come to be regarded as a lyric poem written to commemorate someone's dying.

Lyric poem   is a poem that is designed to express the thoughts, reflections, or feelings of the poet or persona in the poem.

Schools Ugliest Girl Dies

by Albert Garcia

The story we passed
in the halls had her
pinned under a beam,
flames licking
in all directions.
She didn't scream,
the way we told it, just
struggled silently
to free herself.

We laughed. We didn't
know another way
for her death,
so we continued
ranting about her caked hair,
her blotched yellow skin,
and plain green skirts.
*There goes your future
wife*, someone said
to his buddy, and the two
wrestled in the dust
until the bell rang.

I can't speak
for the others, but that day
I began to know the heat
of our valley—a constant
stagnation of air. At home
I walked the orchard,
approached walnut trees,
pretended they were her.
But I couldn't say a thing,
my eyes pinned to sparse grass
in the shade, my mind
burning to recall one time
I didn't avoid the face
that mourned its own
pale skin.

When we read poems in fixed forms, we can know that the poet has offered us something graceful, something constructed with shape, a poem that
is doing its work for us through its foundation, its bedrock. The form is

holding up the content. And while it holds the content, it shapes it, and allows it to flow forth in varying speeds and facades—the way a river bottom, in its gravel or sand or stone, paces the river and creates riffles and runs and windows of water where we see on the surface what lies beneath.

To Experience

1. Choose a form and attempt to write a portion of it in order to see how the lines, meter, and rhyme form in the poem. Try to write four lines of a sonnet. Attempt two stanzas of a villanelle. Give a try to the haiku.

To Write

1. In a short essay or as a journal entry, discuss how the sound differs between a sonnet and a villanelle. Consider how and why the sound causes the subjects in the forms to be handled differently.
2. In a short essay or journal entry, write about how important the function of imagery and metaphor is to the haiku and how that function sets it apart from another form.

Chapter Seven

Reading a Poem
From Page to Mouth to Ear

The history of poetry is oral. Put simply, poetry was meant to be heard. Poems were a pastime, a cultural event, a form of entertainment, which has always been meant to fall on our ears. Even in our most recent past when it seems as if poetry may be getting pushed mostly to the page, it is still meant to be heard. Consider the rise of slam poets and spoken word and performance poets. But we can be sure that even the poems we encounter in book after book and anthology after anthology were written with the intent of being read aloud. The authors wrote them with a sense of rhythm, music, and breath that came out of their own physical being and a sense that they were hearing them as alive words. When I was in college I was trying to read Milton's "Paradise Lost" and having a hard time of it. My professor asked if I was reading aloud, and I told him I hadn't been. He suggested that I go home and read it aloud. So, I began by pacing my living room reading Milton aloud, and by the end I had recruited two other friends. The difference was tremendous as hearing the words brought the text alive and made it more immediately understandable.

"Whether I'm going to perform a poem or not, I always have to hear it out loud, over and over and over. My feeling for the poem is never satisfied on the page. For me there's always something about poetry that just has *to be heard."*

Sekou Sundiata

Part of what happened those days reading "Paradise Lost" aloud, was that I was forced to pay attention to the poetic nuances of the language, mostly the meter, rhythm, and rhyme. These elements of the poem helped the content rise to the surface. Rhythm is something that must be heard and when we pay attention to the rhythm and music of a poem, then the pattern of the language can be heard. And the pattern, especially the rhythmic pattern, of a poem is deeply rooted in what and how the poem means. We read the words in their order, or disorder, but we read them the way they were intended to come to us. We read them in the manner they are linked. When we read silently to ourselves, we have the ability—and we take this opportunity—to stop and ponder, to reread a line, to consider a word or an image. But when we read aloud for ourselves or a group, we read from start to finish allowing the poem to take shape as a unit without interruption—when we read aloud, the poem isn't becoming something through analysis or critical interpretation, the poem simply *is*. This means that the poem can take on its poetic qualities without having them broken down by the reader. The poem can take its cosmic shape, its creative shape and/or space, and it can carry its full evocative power to us. We will come to meet the poem in a place without the barrier of analysis or intent, but rather we might find a word working on us without knowing why intellectually. It's simply that the word or image has stuck in our craw. Maybe the music we hear under the poem is finding some secret place within us because the language is approximating, in many ways, some human feeling we have or have had. That is the alive experience of reading.

The aural experience of reading and listening to a poem is not only significant to our emotional reactions to the poem but our intellectual responses too. In bridging the gap between the sides of present debate whether poetry should be "performance" or "academic," consider that in order for poetry to get into our consciousness, into our blood, we need to hear it first. A poem needs to be able to rise from the page, to sing, to be sung, to fly into the air before we might even consider analyzing it. And if we listen to the poem as readers, we'll hear things that we might analyze later, core pieces of a poem, nuances of a writer's style, part of the collective rhythm to an author's voice, which rises out of the city or region from which they come. We might begin to note how much jazz there is behind Gwendolyn Brooks' poems. And if we collect these pieces, we can build them into a large analytical approach to a poet and poems. For example, if we approach a poet and her poems with phenomenology theory, we may wish to discover and study the particular cadences and nuances to how and why a writer's rhythms exist and work in their poetry.

But aside from the theoretical approach, we know that a poem will exist for us initially and maybe thereafter by how it is read—how we hear it and how we present it if we're the reader. Our goal is to bring the poem into action. We want our voice to be the water that re-hydrates the poem right off the page, which turns it into something living. So, following are some general tips on reading a poem out loud and then a few poems to read and hear.

To Read Aloud

1. *Never read cold.* Give yourself some time to go over the poem. Hopefully, in class, you've been assigned a poem a night or two before you might get called on in class to read. But sometimes class discussions take shape organically and the professor says, "Alright, let's look at this poem on page 141. Anita, will you read it, please?" And Anita ought to say, "Sure. Can I have a minute to look over it?" Once Anita has read the poem to herself and noted spots where there might be difficulty or words she may not know, she could ask about these or look up words before she sets out reading.

2. *Read Slowly.* Often when we read in front of others, we read faster than we would to ourselves or in front of those we're close to. Even very experienced readers do this. Reading a poem slowly will not only allow the listeners to follow and catch important images, ideas, and rhythmic nuances, but it will allow the reader time to work comfortably through any difficult, uncomfortable, or troubled spots in the poem. Reading slowly will also allow the reader to pay close attention to single words, something important to poetry. So, in order to set yourself up for slow reading, give a two or three second pause between the title and first line of the poem. This allows a slow, paced entry.

3. *Read loudly enough for the entire room to hear you.* This can be difficult depending on how large the room is, but you might try standing or borrowing the podium, lectern, or table from your professor. That will allow your voice to carry out to everyone in the room. And project your voice as if you're trying to make certain that an imaginary person sitting behind even the last person in the room can hear you.

4. *Start with the title.* The title is the first line of the poem, so be sure to always read the title. It's also often a signifier for what the poem will be about.

5. *Read with a normal voice and tone.* There's no need to affect your voice or give a dramatic reading of a poem, even if you've heard people do this. Read a poem the way you might read anything else to those around you. Because poets have often focused on specific words carrying weight or doing work for the poem, let the naturalness of the language come out and let the language work for you.

6. *Read with conviction.* I always, somewhat jokingly, tell my students, the poem ought to at the least appear to the audience that it means something to you and that you fully understand it. We may not entirely understand it from a theoretical or analytical perspective when we read it, but at best we might understand how it functions on the page in a rhythmic sense and what places in the poem seem important in a linguistic sense.

7. *Read with the punctuation not necessarily the lines.* While you ready yourself to read, and while you read, be guided by the punctuation of the language. Obviously, as we've discussed before, one of the conventions of poetry is line structure, but if we read by giving a pause at the end of each line we will in most cases read with awkward and unnatural pauses that may also affect the rhythm of the language. We assess meter and rhyme, and allow it to occur in the poem as the lines, punctuation, and rhythm guide us. But we need not emphasize or overemphasize any of these. For example, end-stopped lines that are also end rhyme naturally emphasize the rhyme through their structure. But lines that have end rhyme with no ending punctuation can be read through without stopping or pausing at the end to emphasize the rhyme. Therefore the rhyme takes on a more subtle quality in the poem.

These are seven tips that may help you feel more comfortable reading poetry aloud. And hopefully these tips also assist in allowing the language to take on a natural quality as it meets a room of listeners. Try reading the following poems out loud and note the movement of rhythm and pace and power the language directs in each poem.

homage to my hips
by Lucille Clifton

these hips are big hips
they need space to
move around in.
they don't fit into little
petty places. these hips
are free hips.
they don't like to be held back.
these hips have never been enslaved,
they go where they want to go
they do what they want to do.
these hips are mighty hips.
these hips are magic hips.
i have known them
to put a spell on a man and
spin him like a top!

No Longer Mourn for Me
by William Shakespeare

No longer mourn for me when I am dead
Than you shall hear the surly sullen bell
Give warning to the world that I am fled
From this vile world, with vilest worms to dwell.
Nay, if you read this line, remember not
The hand that writ it, for I love you so
That I in your sweet thoughts would be forgot
If thinking on me then should make you woe.
O, if, I say, you look upon this verse
When I perhaps compounded am with clay,
Do not so much as my poor name rehearse,
But let your love even with my life decay,
       Lest the wise world should look into your moan
       And mock you with me after I am gone.

A Poem for "Magic"
by Quincy Troupe

For Earvin "Magic" Johnson, Donnell Reid & Richard Franklin

take it to the hoop, "magic" Johnson
take the ball dazzling down the open lane
herk & jerk & raise your six feet nine inch
frame into air sweating screams of your neon name
"magic" Johnson, nicknamed "windex" way back in high school
cause you wiped glass backboards so clean
where you first juked & shook
wiled your way to glory
a new style fusion of shake & bake energy
using everything possible, you created your own space
to fly through—any moment now, we expect your wings
to spread feathers for that spooky take-off of yours—
then shake & glide, till you hammer home
a clotheslining deuce off the glass
now, come back down with a reverse hoodoo gem
off the spin, & stick it in sweet, popping nets, clean
from twenty feet, right-side

put the ball on the floor, "magic"
slide the dribble behind your back, ease it deftly
between your bony, stork legs, head bobbing everwhichaway
up & down you see everything on the court

off the high yoyo patter, stop & go dribble, you shoot
a threading needle rope pass, sweet home to kareem
cutting through the lane, his sky hook pops cords
now lead the fastbreak, hit worthy on the fly
now, blindside a behind the back pinpointpass for two more
off the fake, looking the other way
you raise off balance into space
sweating chants of your name, turn, 180 degrees
off the move, your legs scissoring space, like a swimmer's
yo-yoing motion, in deep water, stretching out now toward free
flight, you double pump through human trees, hang in place
slip the ball into your left hand

then deal it like a las vegas card dealer
off squared glass, into nets, living up to your singular nickname
so "bad" you cartwheel the crowd towards frenzy
wearing your electric smile, neon as your name

in victory, we suddenly sense your glorious uplift
your urgent need to be champion
& so we cheer rejoicing with you, for this quicksilver, quicksilver
                                                  quicksilver

moment of fame, so put the ball on the floor again, "magic"
juke & dazzle, shake & bake down the lane
take the sucker to the hoop, "magic" Johnson,
recreate reverse hoodoo gems off the spin,
deal alley-oop-dunk-a-thon-magician passes
now double-pump, scissor, vamp through space
hang in place & put it all up in the sucker's face, "magic"
johnson, & deal the roundball like the jujuman that you am
like the sho-nuff shaman man that you am
"magic," like the sho-nuff spaceman you am

To Experience

1. Study the persona of a poem until you believe you know that character like a real person. Then read the poem how you think that persona would read it.

To Write

1. Choose a poem and read it aloud. Have someone else read it aloud too. Then in a short essay or journal entry discuss what you believe happens to the poem and our experience with it when read aloud rather than silently and why this happens.

Chapter Eight

Writers on Writing
Some Thoughts about Poetry

One way we can learn about poetry is to listen to the varied voices behind the poems we read. As much as we may listen to the voices during poems, writers have some of the most invaluable things to say about their craft when it comes to reading, understanding, and analyzing poetry. They may offer us insight into how to read, how to understand poetry, or how to apply given theories of poetics. As you read some of the following thoughts about poetry, you may find it interesting to reflect them off of some poem you've read that you particularly liked, found interesting, or maybe even a poem that confused you. Quite possibly one of these quotes might offer new or added insight into the poem.

On the Word, Style, and the Poem

"Proper words in proper places, make the true definition of style."

Jonathan Swift

"Of its own accord my song would come in the right rhythms, and what I was trying to say was poetry."

Ovid

"The things that concern you most can't be put in prose. In prose, the tendency is to avoid inner responsibility. Poetry is the discovery of the legend of one's youth."

Theodore Roethke

"I never find words right away. Poems for me always begin with images and rhythms, shapes, feelings, forms, dances in the back of my mind. And much of the poem is already dancing itself out before I start to look around for the words for it. So, I'm not a language poet in the sense that some people say all poetry starts with language. For me language comes *after* imagination. My imagination is pre-linguistic, pre-verbal. In the sense that when you roam around in the spaces of your mind, you're not forming sentences and reeling out vocabulary, you're just looking. You're looking at the landscape of your mind and you're solving problems."

Gary Snyder

"Poetry is oral; it is not words, but words performed . . . the *real* poem is not the scratches on the paper, but the sounds those scratches stand for."

Judson Jerome

"A revelation of the full range of human response to the world—that is what it means to be human on earth. That seems to be what hope is about in relation to art."

Margaret Atwood

"In organic poetry, the metric movement, the measure, is the direct expression of the movement of perception. And the sounds, acting together with the measure, are a kind of extended onomatopoeia— that is they imitate not the sounds of the experience (which may well be soundless, or to which sounds contribute only incidentally) but the feeling of an experience, its emotional tone, its texture."

Denise Levertov

"The anecdotal, the documentary of the human, is not poetic in itself. I proclaim the right of the lyric to *relate* pure emotion, eliminating the totality of the human anecdote."

Antonio Machado

On the Poet

"Artists are the antennae of the race, but the bullet-headed many will never learn to trust their great artists."

Ezra Pound

"My Catholic Girlhood taught me two disciplines that I think are invaluable, I think, for writing: the daily examination of conscience and the meditation on holy pictures."

Marina Warner

"The business of the poet is to show the sorriness underlying the grandest things, and the grandeur underlying the sorriest things."

Thomas Hardy

"A result which is sensational is implemented by what to the craftsman was private and unsensational."

Marianne Moore

"[A] requisite in our poet or maker is imitation, *imitatio,* to be able to convert the substance or riches of another poet to his own use. To make choice of one excellent man above the rest, and so to follow him. . . . Not as a creature that swallows what it takes in, crude raw and undigested; but that feeds with an appetite, and hath a stomach to concoct, divide, and turn all into nourishment."

Ben Jonson

"Words are always getting conventionalized to some secondary meaning. It is one of the works of poetry to take the truants into custody and bring them back to their right senses. Poets are the policemen of language, always arresting those old reprobates, the words."

W.B. Yeats

"The multiplicity of nations and cultures in the word makes it inevitable that the details and particulars of human experience will vary according to time, place, and circumstance, and it follows that the majority of writers will dramatize and interpret human life according to usages of their particular nation and epoch."

Onwuchekwa Jemie

On The Reader and Reading

"The only end of writing is to enable the readers better to enjoy life, or better to endure it."

Samuel Johnson

"We may read poems because we are interested in the poet as a biographical creature who existed in a historical and cultural context, but mostly we read poems because we are curious about ourselves."

Billy Collins

"There is great energy released just by the act of being receptive to words. The poet David Ignatow has talked about keeping the door open—it could be a door in a relationship or a door between the poet and words so that words can come through—and I believe that when you regularly make yourself available to words, they come through more readily for you."

Naomi Shihab Nye

"There is that tradition in Chinese poetry that a poem is a model of the psyche. Psyche is a model of the cosmos, and so a poem is a model, or an instance of the cosmos. It's a little instance of cosmic presence. The Chinese, especially the T'ang and Sung Chinese poets, believe that the poem is an object through which to contemplate or experience cosmic presence. I happen to feel that's true."

Li Young Lee

"The reader must not sit back and expect the poet to do all the work."

Edith Sitwell

"Everything which opens out to us a new world is bound to appear strange at first."

Edith Sitwell

"The process of reading is not a half-sleep. . . . The reader is to do something himself, must be on the alert, must himself or herself construct indeed the poem, the argument, the history—the text furnishing the hints, the clue, the start or framework."

Walt Whitman

The Purpose, Power, and Function of Poetry

"By making us stop for a moment, poetry gives us an opportunity to think about ourselves as human beings on this planet and what we mean to each other. In that way, poetry becomes a voice to power that says, 'Power is not the end-all or be-all.' Equally important is the connection poetry emphasizes of human being to human being: what *are* we doing to make the lives of everyone better, and not just materially, but spiritually as well? I think that's why poetry has often been considered dangerous."

Rita Dove

". . . to me an important part of the business world is trying to get through the macho veneer we've built around business and get to the feelings which are at the heart of business. I keep saying business is life, life is business, so where did we get this macho, tough-guy stuff? In fact, you spend, sixty percent of your waking hours on the job—you celebrate, you suffer, you worry, you feel anxiety and pain and fear and jealousy and joy right there in the workplace every day—and that is what I try to get into poetry. In a way, what I'm saying is that if we deal with the humanity of business, then the business will take care of itself."

James A. Autry

"People are beginning to understand that especially in poetry feeling transcends boundaries of race, culture, class, economics. They are also beginning to understand that intellect does *not* do that. On the other hand, the way we feel, the way we fear, the way we love, the way we hope—these are the same kinds of things for all of us. So poetry that is both intellectual and intuitive seems to me to be poetry that will get past any of the artificial boundaries which separate us."

Lucille Clifton

"A poem should not mean, but be."

Archibald MacLeish

"A poem begins with a lump in the throat; a home sickness or a love sickness. It is a reaching-out toward expression; and effort to find fulfillment. A complete poem is one where an emotion has found its thought and the thought has found the words. My definition of poetry (if I were forced to give one) would be this: words that have become deeds."

Robert Frost

"I think the mission of poetry is to create among people the possibility of wonder, admiration, enthusiasm, mystery, the sense that life is marvelous. When you say that life is marvelous, you are saying a banality. But to make life a marvel—that is the role of poetry."

Octavio Paz

"When I went back to my village, fifty years later, I was not really accepted there either. I can't blame them. Fifty years later *is* a long time! And I must have looked pretty white to them, just as I looked very Indian to the children outside. It took me a while to realize that I am a bridge between both cultures . . . [Poetry] helped me to see that I just did not hate anyone and to write about these things without any bias."

Mary Tall Mountain

On the Canon, Tradition, and Women

"I believe in the established canon of English and American literature and in the validity of the concept of privileged texts. I think it is more important to read Spenser, Shakespeare, or Milton than to read Borges in translation, or even, to say the truth, to read Virginia Woolf."

J. Hillis Miller

"Western Culture . . . was a grand ancestral property that educated men had inherited from their intellectual forefathers, while their female relatives, like characters in a Jane Austen novel, were relegated to modest dower houses on the edge of the estate."

Sandra Gilbert

"Men have had every advantage of us in telling their own story. Education has been theirs in so much higher a degree; the pen has been in their hands."

Jane Austen

"*All* women, as authors, are feeble and tiresome. I wish they were forbidden to write, on pain of having their faces deeply sacrificed with an oyster shell."

Nathaniel Hawthorne

"Women must write through their bodies, they must invent the impregnable language that will wreck partitions, classes and rhetorics, regulations and codes, they must submerge, cut through, get beyond the ultimate reserve-discourse, including the one that laughs at the very idea of pronouncing the word 'silence.'"

Helene Cixous

"Well, at least now [women] can say how we feel. We have always known how men feel about us, but now I feel free to write about, let's say, the body of the man I love. We have permission to say what we want about the men we love. . . . And it is important for a woman to be aware of and to recover her own body because we have been told too many times that we were born to make sure that humankind doesn't disappear; we need to have a consciousness of our own selves and our own bodies."

Daisy Zamora

To Experience

1. Choose one or two of the categories in this chapter and write a two to five sentence quote of your own that might stand alongside the rest of the quotes in the section.

To Write

1. Use a quote from one of the categories and apply the quote to a poem as a thesis for an essay or journal topic.

Chapter Nine

Poems for Further Reading

Snow-Flakes

by Henry Wadsworth Longfellow

Out of the bosom of the air
      Out of the cloud-folds of her garments shaken,
Over the woodlands brown and bare
      Over the harvest-fields forsaken,
      Silent, and soft, and slow
      Descends the snow.

Even as our cloudy fancies take
      Suddenly shape in some divine expression,
Even as the troubled heart doth make
In the white countenance confession
      The troubled sky reveals
      The grief it feels.

This is the poem of the air,
      Slowly in silent syllables recorded;
This is the secret of despair,
      Long in its cloudy bosom hoarded,
      Now whispered and revealed
      To wood and field.

The Passionate Shepherd to His Love

by Christopher Marlowe

Come live with me and be my love,
And we will all the pleasures prove
That valleys, groves, hills, and fields,
Woods, or steepy mountain yields.

And we will sit upon the rocks,
Seeing the shepherds feed their flocks,
By shallow rivers to whose falls
Melodious birds sing madrigals.

And I will make thee beds of roses
And a thousand fragrant posies,
A cap of flowers, and a kirtle
Embroidered all with leaves of myrtle;

A gown made of the finest wool
Which from our pretty lambs we pull;
Fair lined slippers for the cold,
With buckles of the purest gold;

A belt of straw and ivy buds,
With coral clasps and amber studs;
And if these pleasures may thee move,
Come live with me, and be my love.

The shepherds' swains shall dance and sing
For thy delight each May morning:
If these delights thy mind may move,
Then live with me and be my love.

The Pasture
by Robert Frost

I'm going out to clean the pasture spring;
I'll only stop to rake the leaves away
(And wait to watch the water clear, I may):
I shan't be gone long.— You come too.

I'm going out to fetch the little calf
That's standing by the mother. It's so young
It totters when she licks it with her tongue.
I shan't be gone long.— You come too.

Birches
by Robert Frost

When I see birches bend to left and right
Across the lines of straighter darker trees,

I like to think some boy's been swinging them.
But swinging doesn't bend them down to stay
As ice storms do. Often you must have seen them
Loaded with ice a sunny winter morning
After a rain. They click upon themselves
As the breeze rises, and turn many-colored
As the stir cracks and crazes their enamel.
Soon the sun's warmth makes them shed crystal shells
Shattering and avalanching on the snow crust—
Such heaps of broken glass to sweep away
You'd think the inner dome of heaven had fallen.
They are dragged to the withered bracken by the load,
And they seem not to break; though once they are bowed
So low for long, they never right themselves:
You may see their trunks arching in the woods
Years afterwards, trailing their leaves on the ground
Like girls on hands and knees that throw their hair
Before them over their heads to dry in the sun.
But I was going to say when Truth broke in
With all her matter of fact about the ice storm,
I should prefer to have some boy bend them
As he went out and in to fetch the cows—
Some boy too far from town to learn baseball,
Whose only play was what he found himself,
Summer or winter, and could play alone.
One by one he subdued his father's trees
By riding them down over and over again
Until he took the stiffness out of them,
And not one but hung limp, not one was left
For him to conquer. He learned all there was
To learn about not launching out too soon
And so not carrying the tree away
Clear to the ground. He always kept his poise
To the top branches, climbing carefully
With the same pains you use to fill a cup
Up to the brim, and even above the brim.
Then he flung outward, feet first, with a swish,
Kicking his way down through the air to the ground.
So was I once myself a swinger of birches.
And so I dream of going back to be.
It's when I'm weary of considerations.
And life is too much like a pathless wood
Where your face burns and tickles with the cobwebs
Broken across it, and one eye is weeping
From a twig's having lashed across it open.

I'd like to get away from earth awhile
And then come back to it and begin over.
May no fate willfully misunderstand me
And half grant what I wish and snatch me away
Not to return. Earth's the right place for love:
I don't know where it's likely to go better.
I'd like to go by climbing a birch tree,
And climb black branches up a snow-white trunk
Toward heaven, till the tree could bear no more,
But dipped its top and set me down again.
That would be good both going and coming back.
One could do worse than be a swinger of birches.

Because I Could Not Stop for Death

by Emily Dickinson

Because I could not stop for Death—
He kindly stopped for me—
The Carriage held but just Ourselves—
And Immortality.

We slowly drove—He knew no haste
And I had put away
My labor and my leisure too,
For His Civility—

We passed the School, where children strove
At Recess—in the Ring—
We passed the Fields of Grazing Grain—
We passed the Setting Sun

Or rather—He passed Us—
The Dews drew quivering and chill—
For only Gossamer, my Gown—
My Tippet—only Tulle—

We passed before a House that seemed
A Swelling of the Ground—
The Roof was scarcely visible—
The Cornice—in the Ground—

Since then—'tis Centuries—and yet
Feels shorter than the Day
I first surmised the Horses' Heads
Were toward Eternity.

I Think I Could Turn and Live With Animals
by Walt Whitman

I think I could turn and live with animals they are so placid and
self-contained;
I stand and look at them long and long.
They do not sweat and whine about their condition;
They do not lie awake in the dark and weep for their sins;
They do not make me sick discussing their duty to God;
Not one is dissatisfied—not one is demented with the mania of
owning things;
Not one kneels to another, nor to his kind that lived thousands of
years ago;
Not one is respectable or industrious over the whole earth.

Man and Dog on an Early Winter Morning
by Carl Sandburg

There was a tall slough grass
Too tough for the farmers to feed the cattle,
And the wind was sifting through, shaking the grass;
Each spear of grass interfered a little with the wind
And the interference sent up a soft hiss;
A mysterious little fiddler's and whistler's hiss
And it happened all the spears together
Made a soft music in the slough grass.

Too tough for the farmers to cut for fodder.
        "This is a proud place to come to
        On a winter morning, early in winter,"
        Said a hungry man speaking to his dog.
Speaking to himself and the passing wind,
"This is a proud place to come to."

Killers

by Carl Sandburg

I am singing to you
Soft as a man with a dead child speaks;
Hard as a man in handcuffs,
Held where he cannot move:

Under the sun
Are sixteen million men,
Chosen for shining teeth,
Sharp eyes, hard legs,
And a running of young warm blood in their wrists.

And a red juice runs on the green grass;
And a red juice soaks the dark soil.
And the sixteen million are killing. . . and killing and killing.

I never forget them day or night:
They beat on my head for memory of them;
They pound on my heart and I cry back to them,
To their homes and women, dreams and games.

I wake in the night and smell the trenches,
And hear the low stir of sleepers in lines—
Sixteen million sleepers and pickets in the dark:
Some of them long sleepers for always,

Some of them tumbling to sleep to-morrow for always,
Fixed in the drag of the world's heartbreak,
Eating and drinking, toiling . . . on a long job of killing.
Sixteen million men.

A Woman

by Gabriela Mistral
trans. by Doris Dana

Where her house stood, she goes on living
as if it had never burned.
The only words she speaks
are the words of her soul;
to those who pass by she speaks none.

When she says "pine of Aleppo"
she speaks of no tree, but a child;
and when she says "little stream"
or "mirror of gold" she speaks of the same.

When night falls she counts
the charred beams of her house.
Lifting her forehead she sees
the pine of Aleppo stand tall.

(The day lives for its night,
the night for its miracle.)

In every tree, she raises the one
they laid upon the earth.
She warms and wraps and holds him close
to the fire of her breast.

Time Does Not Bring Relief; You All Have Lied
by Edna St. Vincent Millay

Time does not bring relief; you all have lied
Who told me time would ease me of my pain!
I miss him in the weeping of the rain;
I want him at the shrinking of the tide;
The old snows melt from every mountain-side,
And last year's leaves are smoke in every lane;
But last year's bitter loving must remain
Heaped on my heart, and my old thoughts abide!

There are a hundred places where I fear
To go,— so with his memory they brim.
And entering with relief some quiet place
Where never fell his foot or shone his face
I say, "There is no memory of him here!"
And so stand stricken, so remembering him!

Sonnet: 14 "If thou must love me. . . "
by Elizabeth Barrett Browning

If thou must love me, let it be for naught
Except for love's sake only. Do not say

"I love her for her smile—her look—her way
Of speaking gently,— for a trick of thought
That falls in well with mine, and certes brought
A sense of pleasant ease on such a day"—
For these things in themselves, Beloved, may
Be changed, or change for thee,— and love so wrought,
May be unwrought so. Neither love me for
Thine own dear pity's wiping my cheeks dry,—
A creature might forget to weep, who bore
Thy comfort long, and lose thy love thereby!
But love me for love's sake, that evermore
Thou mayst love on, through love's eternity.

In Which She Satisfies a Fear with the Rhetoric of Tears

by Sor Juana Ines de la Cruz
trans. by Willis Barnstone

This afternoon, my love, speaking to you
since I could see that in your face and walk
I failed in coming close to you with talk,
I wanted you to see my heart. Love, who
supported me in what I longed to do,
conquered what is impossible to gain.
Amid my tears that were poured out in pain,
my heart became distilled and broken through.
Enough my love. Don't be so stiff. Don't let
these maddening jealousies and arrogance
haunt you or let your quiet be upset
by foolish shadows: false signs of a man's
presence; and as you see my heart which met
your touch—now it is liquid in your hands.

Manley Hot Springs, Alaska, 1975

by Lisa Chavez

Independence Day and I am twelve,
dark hair falling straight, held back
by a blue bandana. My mother rents a room—
above the lodge's bar—and all night, voices rise
in slurred shouts, while outside,
gunfire rends the air in lieu of fireworks.
From the car, our dog's furious barking.
Darkness never comes, the sun doesn't set.

At five a gunshot in the bar
then shuddering silence.
My mother shifts in her bed. "The dog,"
she says, and I dutifully go to tend to her.
Quiet echoes as I edge down narrow stairs.

On the landing, a bearded man and a rifle
aimed angrily at my face.
"I thought I told all you fucking Indians
to get out of my bar."
My legs shake, wanting to run,
all I can think of is the dog
already maybe peeing on the car's seat;
when I open my mouth, words
rush out with tears—my mom and vacation
and the dog. He doesn't lower the gun,
but opens the door, shoves me out
onto the morning's cool grass.
And I am only twelve. I have never seen
a gun before. I have come from California
where night follows day in orderly fashion,
where on the fourth of July I whirl dizzily
with sparklers in both hands, and place black pellets
on the sidewalk to see them transform
into charcoal snakes. I squeeze my eyes shut,
wish hard for some magic to take me home,
but when I open them, I see only
the unfamiliar spruce, and revelers
swaying unsteadily by. I take the dog
for a walk—I don't know what else to do.

Two young men, Indian, black hair held back
with bandanas like mine, say hello;
I gaze at my feet, whisper a reply.
In the lodge window, I see the gun's
slim shadow, so I crouch by the car
arms tight around the dog's neck, until
she pulls away, shakes herself and stretches.
There is nowhere to go but back.

I try to make myself small,
inoffensive, invisible, but that man
grabs my shoulder hard then lets me go,
rifle still dangling from one hand, an evil

appendage. Cringing like a beat dog, I leap
for the stairs, imagining the rifle raising,
the furious noise, and a sudden sharp
crack in my back.

Hours later, my mother
sends me to breakfast while she searches out
the lodge owner. her voice rises
from another room like bursts of gunfire.
I mop syrup around my plate
with a scrap of blueberry pancake,
stomach tight. The bearded man comes in,
stares hard at me. "She looks like a goddamn Native."
The other diners nod, and I hang
my head, face burning.

Daystar

by Rita Dove

She wanted a little room for thinking:
but she saw diapers steaming on the line,
a doll slumped behind the door.

So, she lugged a chair behind the garage
to sit out the children's naps.

Sometimes there were things to watch—
the pinched armor of a vanished cricket,
a floating maple leaf. Other days
she stared until she was assured
when she closed her eyes
she'd see only her own vivid blood.

She had an hour, at best, before Liza appeared
pouting from the top of the stairs.
And just *what* was mother doing
out back with the field mice? Why,

building a palace. Later
that night when Thomas rolled over and
lurched into her, she would open her eyes

and think of the place that was hers
for an hour—where
she was nothing,
pure nothing, in the middle of the day.

Crossing the Water

by Sylvia Plath

Black lake, black boat, two black, cut-paper people.
Where do the black trees go that drink here?
Their shadows must cover Canada.

A little light is filtering from the water flowers.
Their leaves do not wish us to hurry:
They are round and flat and full of dark advice.

Cold worlds shake from the oar.
The spirit of blackness is in us, it is in the fishes.
A snag is lifting a valedictory, pale hand;

Stars open among the lilies.
Are you not blinded by such expressionless sirens?
This is the silence of astounded souls.

The Colonel

by Carolyn Forche

What you have heard is true. I was in his house. His wife carried a
tray of coffee and sugar. His daughter filed her nails, his son went
out for the night. There were daily papers, pet dogs, a pistol on the
cushion beside him. The moon swung bare on its black cord over the
house. On the television was a cop show. It was in English. Broken
bottles were embedded in the walls around the house to scoop the
kneecaps from a man's legs or cut his hands to lace. On the windows
there were gratings like those in liquor stores. We had dinner, rack of
lamb, good wine, a gold bell was on the table for calling the maid.
The maid brought green mangoes, salt, a type of bread. I was asked
how I enjoyed the country. There was a brief commercial in Spanish.
His wife took everything away. There was some talk then of how
difficult it had become to govern. The parrot said hello on the

terrace. The colonel told it to shut up, and pushed himself from the table. My friend said to me with his eyes: say nothing. The colonel returned with a sack used to bring groceries home. He spilled many human ears on the table. They were like dried peach halves. There is no other way to say this. He took one of them in his hands, shook it in our faces, dropped it into a water glass. It came alive there. I am tired of fooling around he said. As for the rights of anyone, tell your people they can go fuck themselves. He swept the ears to the floor with his arm and held the last of his wine in the air. Something for your poetry, no? he said. Some of the ears on the floor caught this scrap of his voice. Some of the ears on the floor were pressed to the ground.

The Movies

by Florence Kiper Frank

She knows a cheap release
From worry and from pain
The cowboys spur their horses
Over the unending plain.

The tenement rooms are small;
Their walls press on the brain.
Oh, the dip of the galloping horses
On the limitless, wind-swept plain!

Vandal's Moon

by Virgil Suarez

I'm a wandered here, and taking a lamp out past midnight.
I find a pair of egrets startled away, snow-white in flight.
                                        —*Po Chu-I*

So many nights we snuck out, Wasabi and I, to run
down to Tommy's burgers on Alvarado, appease
this late-night hunger of what to do with our lives

in California. We roamed the darkened streets of L.A.
in his father's 70's Nova, a comet blazing in the night.
We rolled down the windows and shouted at the lit

windows—who knew what went on in those rooms,
at that hour? the transvestites staggered out of cheap
hotels and bars, hiking up their skirts at us. Winos

slept in cardboard boxes, which blew away in strong
wind, or did we do it without speed? No cops, no
adult interference. We were barely legal to drive.

We were free, we kept chanting. On full moon nights
if you lived there right in the middle of heaven and hell,
you could see us drive through, two young men, barely

sixteen, hollering up at the vandal's moon. Pure danger
everywhere. Our golden chariot taking us toward light.
We were free, we were free. Filled with moon's delight.

Remember

by Joy Harjo

Remember the sky that you were born under
know each of the star's stories
Remember the moon, know who she is. I met her
in a bar once in Iowa City.
Remember the sun's birth at dawn, that is the
strongest point of time. Remember sundown
and the giving away to night.
Remember your birth, how your mother struggled
to give you form and breath. You are the evidence of
her life, and her mother's, and hers.
Remember your father. He is your life, also.
Remember the earth whose skin you are:
red earth, black earth, yellow earth, white earth
brown earth, we are earth.
Remember the plants, trees, animal life who all have their
tribes, their families, their histories, too. Talk to them,
listen to them. They are alive poems.
Remember the wind. Remember her voice. She knows the
origin of this universe. I heard her singing Kiowa war
dance songs at the corner of Fourth and Central once.
Remember that you are all people and that all people
are you.
Remember that you are this universe and that this
universe is you.
Remember that all is in motion, is growing, is you.
Remember that language comes from this.
Remember the dance that language is, that life is.
Remember.

Uncertain Admission

by Frances Bazil

The sky looks down on me in aimless blues
The sun glares at me with a questioning light
The mountains tower over me with the uncertain shadows
The trees sway in the bewildered breeze
The deer dance in perplexed rhythms
The ants crawl around me in untrusting circles
The birds soar above me with doubtful dips and dives
They all, in their own way, ask the question,
Who are you, who are you?
I have to admit to them, to myself,
I am an Indian.

Spring and All

by William Carlos Williams

By the road to the contagious hospital
under the surge of the blue
mottled clouds driven from the
northeast—a cold wind. Beyond, the
waste of broad, muddy fields
brown with dried weeds, standing and fallen

patches of standing water
and scattering of tall trees

All along the road the reddish
purplish, forked, upstanding, twiggy
stuff of bushes and small trees
with dead, brown leaves under them
leafless vines—

Lifeless in appearance, sluggish
dazed spring approaches—

They enter the new world naked,
cold, uncertain of all
save that they enter. All about them
the cold, familiar wind—

Now the grass, tomorrow
the stiff curl of wildcarrot leaf

One by one objects are defined—
It quickens: clarity, outline of leaf

But now the stark dignity of
entrance—Still, the profound change
has come upon them: rooted, they
grip down and begin to awaken

A Blessing

by James Wright

Just off the highway to Rochester, Minnesota,
Twilight bounds softly forth on the grass.
And the eyes of those two Indian ponies
Darken with kindness.
They have come gladly out of the willows
To welcome my friend and me.
We step over the barbed wire into the pasture
Where they have been grazing all day, alone.
They ripple tensely, they can hardly contain their happiness
That we have come.
They bow shyly as wet swans. They love each other.
There is no loneliness like theirs.
At home once more,
They begin munching the young tufts of spring in the darkness.
I would like to hold the slenderer one in my arms,
For she has walked over to me
And nuzzled my left hand.
She is black and white,
Her mane falls wild on her forehead,
And the light breeze moves me to caress her long ear
That is delicate as the skin over a girl's wrist.
Suddenly I realize
That if I stepped out of my body I would break
Into blossom.

Song

by Laetetia Elizabeth Landon (LEL)

WHERE, O! where's the chain to fling,
One that will bind CUPID's wing,
One that will have longer power
Than the April sun or shower?

From it not of Eastern gold,
All too weighty it to hold;
Form it neither all of bloom,
Never does love find a tomb
Sudden, soon, as when he meets
Death amid unchanging sweets:
But if you would fling a chain,
And not fling it all in vain,
Like a fairy from a spell
Of all that is changeable,
Take the purple tints that deck,
Meteorlike, the peacock's neck;
Take the many hues that play
On the rainbow's colour'd way;
Never let a hope appear
Without its companion fear;
Only smile to sigh, and then
Change into a smile again;
Be to-day as sad, as pale,
As minstrel with his lovelorn tale;
But to-morrow gay as all

The Dreaming Child

by Felicia Dorothea Hemans

Alas! what kind of grief should thy years know?
Thy brow and cheek are smooth as waters be
When no breath troubles them.

BEAUMONT AND FLETCHER

AND is there sadness in *thy* dreams, my boy?
What should the cloud be made of?— blessed child!
Thy spirit, borne upon a breeze of joy,
All day hath ranged through sunshine, clear, yet mild:

And *now* thou tremblest!— wherefore?— in *thy* soul
There lies no past, no future.— Thou hast heard
No sound of presage from the distance roll,
Thy heart bears traces of no arrowy word.

From thee no love hath gone; thy mind's young eye
Hath look'd not into Death's, and thence become

A questioner of mute Eternity,
A weary searcher for a viewless home:

Nor hath thy sense been quicken'd unto pain,
By feverish watching for some step beloved;
Free are thy thoughts, an ever-changeful train,
Glancing like dewdrops, and as lightly moved.

Yet now, on billows of strange passion toss'd,
How art thou wilder'd in the cave of sleep!
My gentle child! 'midst what dim phantoms lost,
Thus in mysterious anguish dost thou weep?

Awake! they sadden me—those early tears,
First gushings of the strong dark river's flow,
That *must* o'ersweep thy soul with coming years
Th' unfathomable flood of human woe!

Awful to watch, ev'n rolling through a dream,
Forcing wild spray-drops but from childhood's eyes!
Wake, wake! as yet *thy* life's transparent stream
Should wear the tinge of none but summer skies.

Come from the shadow of those realms unknown,
Where now thy thoughts dismay'd and darkling rove;
Come to the kindly region all thine own,
The home, still bright for thee with guardian love.

Happy, fair child! that yet a mother's voice
Can win thee back from visionary strife!—
Oh! shall *my* soul, thus waken'd to rejoice,
Start from the dreamlike wilderness of life?

To the Nightingale

by Anne Finch, Countess of Winchilsea

EXERT thy voice, sweet harbinger of spring!
  This moment is thy time to sing,
  This moment I attend to praise,
And set my numbers to thy lays.
  Free as thine shall be my song,
  As thy music, short or long.

Poets wild as thou were born,
   Pleasing best when unconfined,
   When to please is least designed,
Soothing but their cares to rest.
   Cares do still their thoughts molest,
   And still th' unhappy poet's breast,
Like thine, when best he sings, is placed against a thorn.

She begins. Let all be still!
   Muse, thy promise now fulfil!
Sweet, oh sweet, still sweeter yet!
Can thy words such accents fit,
Canst thou syllables refine,
Melt a sense that shall retain
Still some spirit of the brain,
Till with sounds like these it join?
   'Twill not be! then change thy note;
   Let division shake thy throat.
Hark! division now she tries;
Yet as far the Muse outflies.
   Cease then, prithee, cease thy tune.
   Trifler, wilt thou sing till June?
Till thy business all lies waste,
And the time of building's past!
   Thus we poets that have speech,
Unlike what thy forests teach,
   If a fluent vein be shown
   That's transcendent to our own,
Criticise, reform, or preach,
Or censure what we cannot reach.

To tranquillity

by Charlotte Smith

In this tumultuous sphere, for thee unfit,
   How seldom art thou found—Tranquillity!
   Unless 'tis when with mild and downcast eye
By the low cradles thou delight'st to sit
Of sleeping infants—watching the soft breath,
   And bidding the sweet slumberers easy lie;
Or sometimes hanging o'er the bed of death,
   Where the poor languid sufferer—hopes to die.
O beauteous sister of the halcyon peace!

I sure shall find thee in that heavenly scene
   Where Care and Anguish shall their power resign;
Where hope alike, and vain regret shall cease,
   And Memory—lost in happiness serene,
     Repeat no more—that misery has been mine!

Evening

by Charlotte Smith

Oh! soothing hour, when glowing day,
   Low in the western wave declines,
And village murmurs die away,
   And bright the vesper planet shines;

I love to hear the gale of Even
   Breathing along the new-leaf'd copse,
And feel the freshening dew of Heaven,
   Fall silently in limpid drops.

For, like a friend's consoling sighs,
   That breeze of night to me appears;
And, as soft dew from Pity's eyes,
   Descend those pure celestial tears.

Alas! for those who long have borne,
   Like me, a heart by sorrow riven,
Who, but the plaintive winds, will mourn,
   What tears will fall, but those of Heaven?

Verses Written in a Garden

by Lady Mary Wortley Montague

SEE how that pair of billing doves
With open murmurs own their loves;
And, heedless of censorious eyes,
Pursue their unpolluted joys:
No fears of future want molest
The downy quiet of their nest;

No interest joined the happy pair,
Securely blest in Nature's care,
While her dear dictates they pursue:

For constancy is nature too.
    Can all the doctrine of our schools,
Our moral maxims, our religious rules,
Can learning, to our lives ensure
Virtue so bright, or bliss so pure?
The great Creator's happy hand
Virtue and pleasure ever blends:
In vain the Church and Court have tried
Th' united essence to divide:
Alike they find their wild mistake,
The pedant priest, and giddy rake.
                (Wr. by 1740; pub. 1750)

Annabel Lee

by Edgar Allen Poe

It was many and many a year ago,
    In a kingdom by the sea,
That a maiden there lived whom you may know
    By the name of Annabel Lee;—
And this maiden she lived with no other thought
    Than to love and be loved by me.

I was a child and she was a child,
    In this kingdom by the sea,
But we loved with a love that was more than love—
    I and my Annabel Lee—
With a love that the wingèd seraphs of Heaven
    Coveted her and me.

And this was the reason that, long ago,
    In this kingdom by the sea,
A wind blew out of a cloud by night
    Chilling my Annabel Lee;
So that her highborn kinsman came
    And bore her away from me,
To shut her up in a sepulcher°
    In this kingdom by the sea.

The angels, not half so happy in heaven,
    Went envying her and me:—
Yes! that was the reason (as all men know,
    In this kingdom by the sea)

That the wind came out of the clouds, chilling
　And killing my Annabel Lee.

But our love it was stronger by far than the love
　Of those who were older than we—
　Of many far wiser than we—
And neither the angels in heaven above
　Nor the demons down under the sea
Can ever dissever my soul from the soul
　Of the beautiful Annabel Lee:—

For the moon never beams without bringing me dreams
　Of the beautiful Annabel Lee;
And the stars never rise but I feel the bright eyes
　Of the beautiful Annabel Lee;
And so, all the night-tide, I lie down by the side
Of my darling, my darling, my life and my bride,
　In her sepulcher there by the sea,
　In her tomb by the side of the sea.

To My Dear and Loving Husband
by Anne Bradstreet

If ever two were one, then surely we.
If ever man were lov'd by wife, then thee;
If ever wife was happy in a man,
Compare with me ye women if you can.
I prize thy love more than whole Mines of gold,
Or all the riches that the East doth hold.
My love is such that Rivers cannot quench,
Nor ought but love from thee, give recompence.

Thy love is such I can no way repay,
The heavens reward thee manifold I pray.
Then while we live, in love lets so persever,
That when we live no more, we may live ever.
                                        [*1678*]

Sonnet 29: When in Disgrace with Fortune and Men's Eyes
by William Shakespeare (1564–1616)

When, in disgrace with Fortune and men's eyes,
I all alone beweep my outcast state,

And trouble deaf heaven with my bootless° cries,
And look upon myself and curse my fate,
Wishing me like to one more rich in hope,
Featured like him, like him with friends possessed,
Desiring this man's art and that man's scope,
With what I most enjoy contented least;
Yet in these thoughts myself almost despising,
Haply I think on thee, and then my state,
(Like to the lark at break of day arising)
From sullen earth sings hymns at heaven's gate,
For thy sweet love remembered such wealth brings
That then I scorn to change my state with kings.

On Being Brought from Africa to America

by Phillis Wheatley (1754–1784)

'Twas mercy brought me from my *Pagan* land,
Taught my benighted soul to understand
That there's a God, that there's a *Saviour* too:
Once I redemption neither sought nor knew.
Some view our sable race with scornful eye,
"Their colour is a diabolic die."
Remember, *Christians, Negroes,* black as *Cain,*
May be refin'd, and join th' angelic train.

Sonnets from the Portuguese: Number 43

by Elizabeth Barrett Browning (1806–1861)

How do I love thee? Let me count the ways.
I love thee to the depth and breadth and height
My soul can reach, when feeling out of sight
For the ends of Being and ideal Grace.
I love thee to the level of every day's
Most quiet need, by sun and candelight.
I love thee freely, as men strive for Right;
I love thee purely, as they turn from Praise.
I love thee with the passion put to use
In my old griefs, and with my childhood's faith.

I love thee with a love I seemed to lose
With my lost saints,— I love thee with the breath,

Smiles, tears, of all my life!— and, if God choose,
I shall but love thee better after death.

She's Free!
by Frances E. W. Harper (1825–1911)

How say that by law we may torture and chase
A woman whose crime is the hue of her face?—
With her step on the ice, and her arm on her child,
The danger was fearful, the pathway was wild. . . .
But she's free! yes, free from the land where the slave,
From the hand of oppression, must rest in the grave;
Where bondage and blood, where scourges and chains,
Have placed on our banner indelible stains. . . .

The bloodhounds have miss'd the scent of her way,
The hunter is rifled and foiled of his prey,
The cursing of men and clanking of chains
Make sounds of strange discord on Liberty's plains. . . .
Oh! poverty, danger and death she can brave,
For the child of her love is no longer a slave.

The Poplar Field
by William Cowper (1731–1800)

The poplars are felled, farewell to the shade
And the whispering sound of the cool colonnade.
The winds play no longer, and sing in the leaves,
Nor Ouse on his bosom their image receives.

Twelve years have elapsed since I last took a view
Of my favourite field and the bank where they grew,
And now in the grass behold they are laid,
And the tree is my seat that once lent me a shade.

The blackbird has fled to another retreat
Where the hazels afford him a screen from the heat,
And the scene where his melody charmed me before,
Resounds with his sweet-flowing ditty no more.

My fugitive years are all hasting away,
And I must ere long lie as lowly as they,

With a turf on my breast, and a stone at my head,
Ere another such grove shall arise in its stead.

'Tis a sight to engage me, if any thing can,
To muse on the perishing pleasures of man;
Though his life be a dream, his enjoyments, I see,
Have a being less durable even than he.

Dover Beach

by Matthew Arnold (1822–1888)

The sea is calm tonight.
The tide is full, the moon lies fair
Upon the straits—on the French coast the light
Gleams and is gone; the cliffs of England stand,
Glimmering and vast, out in the tranquil bay.
Come to the window, sweet is the night air!
Only, from the long line of spray
Where the sea meets the moon-blanched land,
Listen! you hear the grating roar
Of pebbles which the waves draw back, and fling,
At their return, up the high strand,
Begin, and cease, and then again begin,
With tremulous cadence slow, and bring
The eternal note of sadness in.

Sophocles long ago
Heard it on the Aegean, and it brought
Into his mind the turbid ebb and flow
Of human misery; we
Find also in the sound a thought,
Hearing it by this distant northern sea.

The Sea of Faith
Was once, too, at the full, and round earth's shore
Lay like the folds of a bright girdle furled.
But now I only hear
Its melancholy, long, withdrawing roar,
Retreating, to the breath
Of the night wind, down the vast edges drear
And naked shingles of the world.

Ah, love, let us be true
To one another! for the world, which seems
To lie before us like a land of dreams,
So various, so beautiful, so new,
Hath really neither joy, nor love, nor light,
Nor certitude, nor peace, nor help for pain;

And we are here as on a darkling plain
Swept with confused alarms of struggle and flight,
Where ignorant armies clash by night.

A Psalm of Life

by Henry Wadsworth Longfellow

Life that shall send
A challenge to its end,
And when it comes, say, 'Welcome, friend.'

What the Heart of the Young Man Said to the Psalmist

I

Tell me not, in mournful numbers,
   Life is but an empty dream!

For the soul is dead that slumbers,
   And things are not what they seem.

II

Life is real—life is earnest—
   And the grave is not its goal:
Dust thou art, to dust returnest,
   Was not spoken of the soul.

III

Not enjoyment, and not sorrow,
   Is our destin'd end or way;
But to *act,* that each to-morrow
   Find us father than to-day.

IV

Art is long, and time is fleeting,
   And our hearts, though stout and brave,

Still, like muffled drums, are beating
   Funeral marches to the grave.

V

In the world's broad field of battle,
   In the bivouac of Life,
Be not like dumb, driven cattle!
   Be a hero in the strife!

VI

Trust no Future, howe'er pleasant!
Let the dead Past bury its dead!
Act—act in the glorious Present!
Heart within, and God o'er head!

VII

Lives of great men all remind us
   We can make *our* lives sublime,
And, departing, leave behind us
   Footsteps on the sands of time.

VIII

Footsteps, that, perhaps another,
   Sailing o'er life's solemn main,
A forlorn and shipwreck'd brother,
   Seeing, shall take heart again.

IX

Let us then be up and doing,
   With a heart for any fate;
Still achieving, still pursuing,
   Learn to labor and to wait.

Ozymandias

by Percy Bysshe Shelley (1792–1822)

I met a traveller from an antique land,
Who said— "Two vast and trunkless legs of stone
Stand in the desert. . . . Near them, on the sand,
Half sunk, a shattered visage lies, whose frown,
And wrinkled lip, and sneer of cold command,
Tell that its sculptor well those passions read
Which yet survive, stamped on these lifeless things,

The hand that mocked them, and the heart that fed;
And on the pedestal, these words appear;
'My name is Ozymandias, King of Kings,
Look on my Works, ye Mighty, and despair!'
Nothing beside remains. Round the decay
Of that colossal Wreck, boundless and bare
The lone and level sands stretch far away."

These verses, songs and poems translated by Frances Densmore

<u>Chippewa</u>
Mide Songs

In form like a bird,
It appears.

The ground trembles
As I am about to enter.
My heart fails me
As I am about to enter
The spirit lodge.

The sound of flowing waters
Comes toward my home.

Now and then there will arise,
Out of the waters,
My Mide brothers,
The otters.

Beautiful as a star,
Hanging in the sky,
Is our Mide lodge.

What are you saying to me?
I am arrayed like the roses,
And beautiful as they.

The sound is fading away.
It is of five sounds.
Freedom.
The sound is fading away.
It is of five sounds.

My Love Has Departed

A loon,
I thought it was.
But it was
My love's
Splashing oar.

Love Song

He must be very sorrowful,
Since he so deceived
And forsook me,
During
My young days.

Teton Sioux
Song on Applying War Paint

At the center of the earth
I stand,
Behold me!
At the wind center
I stand,
Behold me!
A root of medicine
Therefore I stand,
At the wind center
I stand.

Song after Battle

As the young men went by
I was looking for him.
It surprises me anew
That he has gone.
It is something
To which I cannot be reconciled.

Owls hoot at me.
Owls hoot at me.
That is what I hear
In my life.
Wolves howl at me.

Wolves howl at me.
That is what I hear
In my life.

Yuman and Yaqui Songs

The water bug is drawing
The shadows of the evening
Toward him on the water.

In Cocori is a young girl
Whose names is Hesucita.
She is a pretty girl.
Her eyes look like stars.
Her pretty eyes are like stars moving.

The owl was requested
To do as much as he knew how.
He only hooted and told of the morning star.
And hooted again and told of the dawn.

The bush
Is sitting
Under a tree
And singing.

The deer
Looks at a flower.

The City Dead-House

by Walt Whitman

By the City Dead-House, by the gate,
As idly sauntering, wending my way from the clangor,
I curious pause—for lo! an outcast form, a poor dead prostitute brought;
Her corpse they deposit unclaim'd—it lies on the damp brick pavement;
The divine woman, her body—I see the Body—I look on it alone,
That house once full of passion and beauty—all else I notice not;
Nor stillness so cold, nor running water from faucet, nor odors morbific impress me;
But the house alone—that wondrous house—that delicate fair house—that ruin!
That immortal house, more than all the rows of dwellings ever built!

Or white-domed Capitol itself, with majestic figure surmounted—or all the old
high-spired cathedrals;
That little house alone, more than them all—poor, desperate house!
Fair, fearful wreck! tenement of a Soul! itself a Soul!
Unclaim'd, avoided house! take one breath from my tremulous lips;
Take one tear, dropt aside as I go, for thought of you,
Dead house of love! house of madness and sin, crumbled! crush'd!
House of life—erewhile talking and laughing—but ah, poor house! dead, even then;
Months, years, an echoing, garnish'd house—but dead, dead, dead.

The Fiddler of Dooney

by W. B. Yeats

When I play on my fiddle in Dooney,
Folk dance like a wave of the sea;
My cousin is priest in Kilvarnet,
My brother in Moharabuiee.

I passed my brother and cousin:
They read in their books of prayer;
I read in my book of songs
I bought at the Sligo fair.

When we come at the end of time,
To Peter sitting in state,
He will smile on the three old spirits,
But call me first through the gate;

For the good are always the merry,
Save by an evil chance,
And the merry love the fiddle
And the merry love to dance:

And when the folk there spy me,
They will all come up to me,
With 'Here is the fiddler of Dooney!'
And dance like a wave of the sea.

The Tavern
by Edwin Arlington Robinson

Whenever I go by there nowadays
And look at the rank weeds and the strange grass,
The torn blue curtains and the broken glass,
I seem to be afraid of the old place;
And something stiffens up and down my face,
For all the world as if I saw the ghost
Of old Ham Amory, the murdered host,
With his dead eyes turned on me all aglaze.

The Tavern has a story, but no man
Can tell us what it is. We only know
That once long after midnight, years ago,
A stranger galloped up from Tilbury Town,
Who brushed, and scared, and all but overran
That skirt-crazed reprobate, John Evereldown.

A deposition from love
by Thomas Caren

I was foretold, your rebell sex,
Nor love, nor pitty knew;
And with what scorn you use to vex
Poor hearts that humbly sue;
Yet I believ'd, to crown our pain,
Could we the fortress win,
The happy Lover sure should gain
A Paradise within:
I thought Loves plagues, like Dragons sate,
Only to fright us at the gate.

But I did enter, and enjoy
What happy Lovers prove;
For I could kiss, and sport, and toy,
And taste those sweets of love;
Which had they but a lasting state,
Or if in *Celia's* brest

The force of love might not abate,
Jove were too mean a guest.
But now her breach of faith, farre more
Afflicts, than did her scorn before.

Hard fate! to have been once possest,
As victor, of a heart
Atchiev'd with labour, and unrest,
And then forc'd to depart.
If the stout Foe will not resigne
When I besiege a Town,
I lose, but what was never mine;
But he that is cast down
From enjoy'd beauty, feels a woe,

Only deposed Kings can know.

The Song of the Foot-Track

by Elsie Cole

Come away, come away from the straightness of the road;
    I will lead you into delicate recesses
Where peals of ripples ring through the maidenhair's abode
    In the heart of little water wildernesses.

I will show you pleasant places; tawny hills the sun has kissed,
    Where the giant trees the wind is always swinging
Rise from clouds of pearly saplings tipped with rose and
amethyst,—
    Fairy boughs where fairy butterflies are clinging.

Come away from the road; I will lead through shade and sheen,
    Changing brightly as the year of colour passes
Through each tint the opal knows, from the flaming winter green
    To the summer gold and silver of the grasses.

Here is riot of leaf and blossom, ferny mosses in the glade
    Pressing round the wattle's stem of dappled splendour;
Even the pathway that you tread smiles with daisies unafraid,—
    Laden branches lean to breathe a welcome tender.

Come away from the road; let wild petals cool your eyes
    Dim and hardened with the arid light of duty;

Lose awhile your weary purpose, leave the highway of the wise
　For the little reckless of joy and beauty.

I am fairer still to follow where the Bush is lonelier grown
　And the purple vines fling tendrils out to bind me;
For the secret of my lure is the call of the Unknown,
　Hidden Loveliness that laughs: '*Come and find me!*'

Follow on, ah, come with me! Though the way is fainter shown
　Where the restless waves of green have splashed and crossed me;
In the temple of the trees you have met delight alone;
　Winning happiness, what matter though you lost me?

In this dreamy fane of sunshine, where wood-violets are rife,
　Though I leave you,— path and bracken surges blended,—
Would you say I led you vainly? I have sung the joy of life,
　I have set you in the way; my song is ended.

Cradle Song

by Louis Esson

Baby, O baby, fain you are for bed,
　Magpie to mopoke busy as the bee;
The little red calf's in the sung cow-shed,
　An' the little brown bird's in the tree.

Daddy's gone a-shearin', down the Castlereagh,
　So we're all alone now, only you an' me.
All among the wool-O, keep your wide blades full-O!
　Daddy thinks o'baby, wherever he may be.

Baby, my baby, rest your drowsy head,
　The one man that works here, tired you must be,
The little red calf's in the snug cow-shed,
　An' the little brown bird's in the tree.

Homesick

by Dorothy Frances McCrae

I'm sick of fog and yellow gloom,
　Of faces strange, and alien eyes,
Your London is a vault, a tomb,
　To those born 'neath Australian skies.

O land of gold and burning blue,
I'm crying like a child for you!

The trees are tossing in the park
   Against the banked-up amethyst,
At four o'clock it will be dark,
   And I a blind man in the mist.
Hark to old London's smothered roar,
Gruff jailer growling at my door!

Each day I see Fate's wheel whirl round,
   And yet my fortunes are the same,
My hopes are trodden in the ground,
   Good luck has never heard my name,
O friends, O home, beyond the seas,
Alone in darkness here I freeze!

The day is dead: night falls apace;
   I reach my hand to draw the blind,
To hide old London's frowning face,
   And then (alas) I call to mind
The shining ways we used to roam
Those long, light evenings at home.

I hate this fog and yellow gloom,
   These days of grey and amethyst;
I want to see the roses bloom,
The smiling fields by sunshine kissed—
O land of gold and burning blue!
I'm crying like a child for you!

The New Life

by Witter Bynner

Perhaps they laughed at Dante in his youth,
Told him that truth
Had unappealably been said
In the great masterpieces of the dead:—
Perhaps he listened and but bowed his head
In acquiescent honour, while his heart
Held natal tidings,— that a new life is the part
Of every man that's born,

A new life never lived before,
And a new expectant art;
It is the variations of the morn
That are forever, more and more,
The single dawning of the single truth.
So answers Dante to the heart of youth!

A Winter Ride

by Amy Lowell

Who shall declare the joy of the running!
   Who shall tell of the pleasures of flight!
Springing and spurning the tufts of wild heather,
   Sweeping, wide-winged, through the blue dome of light.
Everything mortal has moments immortal,
   Swift and God-gifted, immeasurably bright.

So with the stretch of the white road before me,
   Shining snow crystals rainbowed by the sun,
Fields that are white, stained with long, cool, blue shadows,
   Strong with the strength of my horse as we run.
Joy in the touch of the wind and the sunlight!
   Joy! With the vigorous earth I am one.

POETRY CREDITS

Chapter 1:

"Green Chile" by Jimmy Santiago Baca, from BLACK MESA POEMS, copyright © 1989 by Jimmy Santiago Baca. Reprinted by permission of New Directions Publishing Corp.

James Wright, "A Blessing" and "Lying in a Hammock at William Duffy's Farm in Pine Island, Minnesota" from THIS BRANCH WILL NOT BREAK, © 1963 by James Wright and reprinted by permission of Wesleyan University Press.

Chapter 2:

Gary Soto, "Oranges" from NEW AND SELECTED POEMS by Gary Soto. Published by Chronicle Books, San Francisco, LLC. Used with permission.

Huang Pien, "Cups of Jade" from THE HUNDRED NAMES, Henry Hart, trans., 1933, University of California Press. Copyright © 1933 The Regents of the University of California. Reprinted by permission.

"Axe Handles" from AXE HANDLES by Gary Snyder. Copyright © 1983 by Gary Snyder. Reprinted by permission of North Point Press, a division of Farrar, Straus and Giroux, LLC.

Jim Harrison, "March Walk" from THE SHAPE OF THE JOURNEY: NEW AND COLLECTED POEMS. Copyright © 1998 by Jim Harrison. Reprinted with the permission of Copper Canyon Press, P.O. Box 271, Port Townsend, WA 98368-0271.

Chapter 3:

"Marks." Copyright © 1978 by Linda Pastan, from PM/AM: New and Selected Poems by Linda Pastan. Used by permission of W.W. Norton & Company, Inc.

"What Work Is" from WHAT WORK IS by Philip Levine, copyright © 1992 by Philip Levine. Used by permission of Alfred A. Knopf, a division of Random House, Inc.

Sekou Sundiata, "Blink Your Eyes" is reprinted by kind permission of Sekou Sundiata.

"Poem for the Young White Man Who Asked Me How I, an Intelligent Well-Read Person Could Believe in the War Between Races" from EPLUMADA, by Lorna Dee Cervantes, © 1981. Reprinted by permission of the University of Pittsburgh Press.

Chapter 4:

"Dream Deferred" from THE COLLECTED POEMS OF LANGSTON HUGHES by Langston Hughes, copyright © 1994 by The Estate of Langston Hughes. Used by permission of Alfred A. Knopf, a division of Random House, Inc.

GLOSSARY

Alliteration   is the repetition of consonant sounds that usually occurs at the beginning of words and produces an echo effect thereby linking words through their sounds.

Ambiguity   in poetry is when a word, group of words or line(s) has multiple literal and figurative meanings.

Assonance   is the repetition of vowel sounds in words and also produces an effect similar to alliteration or consonance. It is a partial rhyme. The vowel sounds are the same, but the consonant sounds may differ.

Cacophony   is when a word (or words) produces a noisy or unpleasant effect. This may happen from the true sound of the word, the word's meaning, or it may happen based on the rhythm of line structure and/or word groupings.

Caesura   is a pause within a line, usually occurring because of punctuation, that breaks the regularity of the rhythmic or metrical pattern.

Consonance   is the repetition of consonant sounds in closely placed words.

Context   is an overall sense of what's happening in a poem, what meaning or forces are being constructed in either the whole poem or part of a poem.

Controlling metaphor   extends itself throughout an entire poem and becomes the controlling force behind the poem, the context by which we come to understand the poem.

Couplet   is a two-line stanza.

Elegy   has come to be regarded as a lyric poem written to commemorate someone's dying.

Enjambment   is when a sentence, or sense of a phrase, does not stop at the end of a line in either its grammatical sense or its meaning.

Euphony   is the blending of sounds into a pleasurable effect on the ear. This may happen from the true sound of the word, the word's meaning, or it may happen based on the rhythm of line structure and/or word groupings.

Falling meter   is when a foot moves from stressed to unstressed syllables.

Fixed form   poem is one that conforms to a set pattern of lines, stanzas, rhyme, and/or meter designated by a fixed structure for a poem.

Foot   is a measurement of stressed and unstressed syllables.

Haiku   is a three line poem consisting of seventeen syllables following a line structure of five, seven, and five syllables and without requirements of rhyme.

Imagery   is a concrete representation of an object, feelings, or ideas using either literal or figurative language associated with our senses.

Implied metaphor   does not actually state in the comparison what our main object is being compared to; rather, it implies the comparison usually through action or ascribing attributes.

Lyric poem   is a short poem that is designed to express the thoughts, reflections, or feelings of the poet or persona.

Metaphor   is a direct comparison of two concrete objects in which one object takes on the characteristics of the other.

Meter   is the arrangement of measured rhythm in poetry and this measurement happens based on where the stressed and unstressed syllables are in words.

Onomatopoeia   is when a word sounds like or resembles what it is. For example, the word hiss actually has a hiss embedded in its sound.

Persona   is the speaker of the poem, the one who takes on the point of view in a poem.

Personification   is giving a nonhuman or inanimate object some human characteristic.

Quatrain   is a four-line stanza.

Rhyme   is an echoing produced by close placement of two or more words with similarly sounding final syllables. There are a number of types of rhyme: there is *masculine rhyme* in which two words end with the same vowel consonant combination (hand/band); *feminine rhyme* in which two syllables rhyme (shiver/liver); *end rhyme* in which the rhyme comes at the end of the lines (this is probably the most commonly used rhyme); and *internal rhyme* in which a word within a line rhymes with another word in that line or at the end or rhymes with a word of similar placement in the following line. There is also a type of rhyme called *slant rhyme* in which the sounds nearly rhyme but are not a "true rhyme" (land/lend). And finally there is what we call *sight rhyme* where the words look alike but do not sound alike (hood/blood).

Rhythm   is the music formed by stressed and unstressed syllables in a line

Rising meter   is when a foot moves from unstressed syllables to stressed syllables.

Sestet   is a six-line stanza.

Simile   is a comparison of two things using the words *like* or *as*.

Sonnet   is a 14 line poem usually set in five foot iambic lines. Rhyme schemes vary between the Italian tradition and the English tradition, largely because of the linguistic possibilities of rhyme, but also because of the slight difference in structure.

Stanza   is a group of two or more lines set together in a poem and often arranged around a metrical, conceptual, or rhythmic pattern.

Symbolism   is an element of imagery whereby meaning is embedded into a poem beneath the literal usage of the words by using a symbol or symbols. A symbol is a concrete object that functions exactly as it *is* but also means or suggests something greater within the context of the poem, wider at an abstract level by reason of relationship or association.

Tercet   is a three-line stanza.

Tone   of a poem is the emotional condition behind the voice of the persona.

Villanelle   consists of nineteen lines divided into six stanzas. There are five tercets (three-line stanzas) and a final quatrain (four-line stanza). The rhyme scheme of the stanzas is *aba* for each of the tercets and *abaa* for the concluding quatrain. Further, the lines repeat in the following order: line one appears in the poem as lines six, twelve, and eighteen; and line three appears in the poem as lines nine, fifteen, and nineteen.

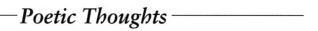 *Poetic Thoughts*

Poetic Thoughts

Poetic Thoughts

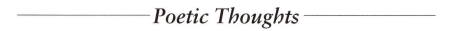

Poetic Thoughts

Poetic Thoughts

Poetic Thoughts